THE NEW TESTAMENT

THE NEW TESTAMENT

Its Writers and Their Messages

BY

C. F. HUNTER, B.A.

Author of
"What a Christian Believes and Why," "Familiar Talks on Sunday School Teaching," "An Introduction to Sunday School Work," etc.

THIRD EDITION, REVISED

LONDON:
METHODIST SUNDAY SCHOOL DEPARTMENT,
LUDGATE CIRCUS HOUSE, E.C.4

Printed in Great Britain by
Wyman & Sons, Ltd., London, Fakenham and Reading.

[illegible].
October, 1942.

PREFACE TO THE THIRD EDITION

At the last revision of this book additions and modifications, necessitated by the advance of New Testament study in the interval since its original publication were made by means of notes in an appendix. The opportunity now arises to revise and reset the book entirely.

Once more I have to acknowledge with deep gratitude the expert guidance and assistance very readily and generously given by Prof. W. F. Howard, M.A., D.D., of Handsworth College, Birmingham. Whilst it must not be supposed that he endorses all the opinions expressed, he has carefully re-read the book and indicated the points at which alteration or addition is now called for as the result of work in this subject in recent years.

The *Supplement to Peake's Commentary* (1936) has also been freely used.

For the convenience of any who may be conducting Classes or Study Circles in which some of the members are using copies of the last edition, it may be said that the principal changes are that the numbered notes in the appendix to the Second Edition have been woven into the text, and slight alterations have been introduced in a number of other places. The most important entirely new additions are the references to modern Synoptic theories on p. 30, and the discussion of the possible Ephesian origin of the Captivity Epistles on pp. 164–68.

An Index has also been added, and a few blank pages for manuscript notes.

C. F. Hunter.

Bramhall, Cheshire, July, 1937.

CONTENTS

CONTENTS

CHAPTER I

How We Got the New Testament

A.—ITS NAME

Our Bible comes to us in two great divisions, the Old and New Testaments. In the first days of Christianity the Old Testament was generally called "The Scriptures," though the full Jewish title was "The Law, the Prophets, and the Writings." When the Christian books were collected together and were regarded as a second volume of Scriptures, it became necessary to distinguish between the two. Seeing that one records the old covenant between God and men made through Moses, and the other the new covenant made through Jesus Christ, one was called "The Old Covenant," the other "The New Covenant." The Greek word for covenant, *dĭăthēkē*, was translated in Latin *testamentum*, and this gave us the English "Testament." Unfortunately we use the word to mean a will, or document by which a man disposes of his property, so that the title is misleading: it ought to be *The New Covenant*.

B.—HOW THE LIST OF BOOKS WAS FIXED

Like the Old Testament, the New Testament is not one book, but a collection of books, or library. These books were written at intervals between about A.D. 50 and 100, though 2 Peter should perhaps be dated even later, and they were written for different Churches, so that it was a long while before some of them became generally known, and longer still before a general understanding was reached as to which should be included in the authoritative collection to be used in all the Churches.

The Canon.—This authoritative list is called the *Canon* of the New Testament, from a Greek word which means a ruler, and then a measure, like our foot-rule, since these books were accepted as the standard for judging Christian truth. The books thus admitted to the New Testament are known as the "canonical books."

Some early lists have come down to us, the most important being the *Muratorian Canon*, found in an ancient manuscript now at Milan and first published in modern form by a man called Muratori in 1740. Some lists were extremely meagre, e.g., *Marcion* (about A.D. 140) rejected all except the Epistles of Paul and a mutilated form of Luke. But Marcion was heretical in many ways and rejected the Old Testament altogether.

Rejected books.—Several interesting books were used in worship in some Churches and almost secured a place in the Canon, but were finally rejected. The most important were: 1. *The Apocalypse of Peter*, of the same type as the Revelation, but not by Peter. 2. *The Gospel of Peter*. Referred to by several of the Fathers. Scholars date it A.D. 130–170. The fragment which has survived is marked by several fantastic additions to the story of the Crucifixion and Resurrection. 3. *The Epistle of Barnabas*, not by Barnabas, Paul's companion. 4. *The Epistle of Clement*, by Clement, Bishop of Rome. 5. *The Shepherd of Hermas*, an allegory called *The Shepherd*, by a teacher called Hermas. 6. *The Teaching of the Twelve Apostles*, or *Didache* (pronounced did-ă-kē), a little book of Christian teaching, probably written about A.D. 110.

Disputed books.—On the other hand, some of the books we now have in our New Testament were not recognized by all the Churches or definitely included in the Canon for a long while, namely: Hebrews, Jude, 2 Peter, 2 and 3 John, James, Revelation.

Note very carefully that the books which are most important for the Christian Faith were all accepted unhesitatingly: the Church had no doubts about including the four Gospels and the thirteen Epistles of Paul that we find in our New Testament. (Hebrews, which was one of the "disputed books," makes no claim to be by Paul, though late forms of the title ascribe it to him.)

Final selection.—Our list of twenty-seven books appears for the first time in the proceedings of the Synod of Laodicea (363), and again in those of the third Council of Carthage (397). The principle followed in making the selection was to include *all books believed to be written by Apostles or their personal disciples*.

C.—THE BOOKS FINALLY INCLUDED

The books of the New Testament may be arranged in certain groups. The names of groups which are printed in italics should be learnt, as they are very frequently used.

1. BIOGRAPHIES OF JESUS.

(*a*) *The Synoptic Gospels*, which give the same view of Jesus: Matthew, Mark, Luke.

(*b*) The supplementary Gospel, written to complete the Synoptics: John.

2. THE STORY OF THE FOUNDING OF THE CHRISTIAN CHURCH: Acts.

3. LETTERS OF PAUL.

(*a*) His earliest Epistles: 1 and 2 Thessalonians.

(*b*) *The Evangelical Epistles*, which set forth the doctrines of salvation: Romans, 1 and 2 Corinthians, Galatians.

(*c*) *The Epistles of the Imprisonment*, written probably from Rome: Ephesians, Colossians, Philippians, Philemon.

(*d*) *The Pastoral Epistles*, written to young colleagues about the work of the Christian pastor or minister: 1 and 2 Timothy, Titus.

4. LETTERS BY OTHER WRITERS.

(*a*) An anonymous Epistle supposed to have some connexion with Paul, though it does not name him, and is not believed to be by him: Hebrews.

(*b*) *The Catholic Epistles*, so called because written to Christians in general or the "Church Catholic": 1 and 2 Peter, James, Jude, 1, 2 and 3 John.

5. NEW TESTAMENT PROPHECY.

The Revelation or *Apocalypse*.

Authorship.—Many of these books make a definite claim to be the work of particular writers, e.g., thirteen of the Epistles claim to be by Paul. Others, e.g., the Gospels and Hebrews, do not name their writers, though an author's name has been attached to each of them by early tradition. Modern scholars, especially those who are less friendly to orthodox Christianity, dispute the traditional view as to the authorship and early date of a number of the books. The most interesting and the most serious of the questions which arise are those connected with the authorship of Matthew, John, the Pastoral Epistles, Hebrews, 2 Peter and the Revelation. These questions are too complicated for full discussion in an elementary textbook, though the more important of them will be treated briefly in due course. Meanwhile it may be said that the great majority of English scholars depart comparatively little from the familiar views.

D.—THE LANGUAGE OF THE NEW TESTAMENT

Greek was the language in general use in our Saviour's day in many parts of the Roman Empire round the Mediterranean seaboard. It was supposed at one time that the Greek of the New Testament was a distinct variety. But during the last few years large numbers of miscellaneous documents belonging to the everyday life of the people, such as family letters and household bills, have been unearthed in the Nile Valley, and these make it clear that the Greek we find in the New Testament was merely the ordinary colloquial Greek of the day. Its vocabulary is smaller than that of Classical Greek, and its grammar less elaborate, so that it differs from Classical Greek in much the same way as the language used by an average Englishman in daily conversation differs from that of Milton's prose works.

E.—HOW WE GOT THE NEW TESTAMENT

Manuscripts.—Until the invention of printing, about 1450, every copy of the New Testament had to be written by hand. Such a manuscript is called a *codex* (plural, *codices*), and the words it contains are called its *text*. The original autographs of the New Testament books have perished, and though some fragmentary pieces of an earlier date have been preserved, the oldest of our great MSS. are hardly older than about A.D. 350. There are two main clues to the age of the MSS.: (1) The material on which they are written is one guide, for *papyrus* (a kind of paper made from the pith of a reed), *vellum* (or parchment) and *cotton-paper* were used at different periods. (2) The character of the writing is another guide, for whilst about seventy old copies or fragments are in detached letters very like capitals and are called *Uncials*, the remaining 2,000 are written in a running hand and are called *Cursives*. Many of the MSS. are known by special names, but they are usually referred to by symbols. The Uncials are indicated by capital letters, e.g., A, B, C, D, א (i.e., Aleph, the first letter of the Hebrew alphabet, pronounced *ah-lĕf*). The Cursives are indicated by numerals, e.g., 17, 389.

The most ancient and valuable of the MSS. are:

א or Aleph, also called *Codex Sinaiticus*. Found by Tischendorf in 1844 in a monastery on Mount Sinai, when some leaves had already been used for lighting fires. He persuaded the monks to present it to the Czar of Russia. It was bought from the Soviet Government, partly by Government funds and partly by private subscription, for the British Museum, in 1934, and can now be seen there.

A or *Codex Alexandrinus*. In the British Museum. Presented to Charles I by his ambassador to Turkey.

B or *Codex Vaticanus*. In the Vatican Library (i.e., the Pope's library) at Rome.

C or the *Palimpsest of Ephraem Syrus*, at Paris. The copy of the N.T. has been washed off and the vellum used again for the writings of a certain Ephraem Syrus. (Note the name *palimpsest* for such MSS. The original writing can generally be deciphered by a skilled reader, and if it is very indistinct it comes out more clearly when the page is photographed.)

D or *Codex Bezae*. At Cambridge. Remarkable for a great number of insertions, some of them very interesting. It contains only the Gospels and Acts.

W, the *Washington Codex*, often called the *Freer MS.*, fourth or fifth century. Bought near Cairo in 1906 by an American, Mr. C. L. Freer. Remarkable for the long form of the conclusion of Mark quoted on p. 45.

Variant Readings.—The copyists were but human, and even a trained man was liable to make mistakes in his work. If these were not corrected, they appeared again in the next copy with additional errors introduced by that copyist, and so the text became less accurate with each successive copying, just as a story becomes less and less like the original each time it is repeated. Hence *the oldest manuscripts, which are the result of few copyings, are much better than later manuscripts, which are the result of many copyings.*

The differences between our copies are called *variant readings* (not "various"). The most important kinds of error are:

1. *Slips made by the copyist.*

(*a*) Omitting a word or part of a word.

(*b*) Writing a word or part of a word twice.

(c) Writing from memory instead of watching the copy.

2. *Intentional alterations.*

(*a*) Changing a word to make the sentence read more smoothly or to make the meaning clearer.

(*b*) Changing a word to make the passage agree with some similar one, e.g., where a saying of Jesus is found in more than one Gospel.

(*c*) In a very few cases changes were introduced to emphasize some doctrine.

3. *Insertions and additions* by weaving into the text some note that had been written in the margin. The R.V. has made us familiar with two striking instances. In John vii. 53–viii. 11 the story of the woman taken in adultery is almost certainly a true story of Jesus, but it is not found in the earliest manuscripts, and was not recorded in the Gospel as John wrote it. Some reader heard it and wrote it in the margin, and the next copyist thought that

he was meant to insert it in the text. Similarly in John v. 4 the words about the angel descending into the pool were not written by John: they state the common belief current in Jerusalem as to the cause of this intermittent spring; some reader noted them in the margin, and the next copyist worked them into the text.

F.—HOW WE GET A CORRECT TEXT

Textual Criticism.—The greater our reverence for the Bible the more important it becomes to make sure that we have the exact words of the inspired writers. The process by which we endeavour to reach a pure text is called *Textual Criticism*, i.e., the critical or exact study of the text. This must be distinguished from the *Higher Criticism*, which is the study of the materials used by a writer in compiling his book. Higher Criticism is like exploring the sources of the River Thames and the various streams that contribute to it. Textual Criticism is like filtering its water when it reaches us in London so as to bring it back to its original purity. The word "higher" is used of the former process because it deals with the stream higher up, at its source.

There are three main departments of this study: (*a*) The examination of the manuscripts. (*b*) The examination of early translations. (*c*) The examination of quotations found in early Christian writings.

1. *The Evidence of the Manuscripts*

General Rules.—Almost incredible labour has been spent on the minute comparison of the MSS.

With some 2,000 copies to work upon, the total number of variant readings tabulated is enormous. The immense majority of these, however, are easily accounted for and may be dismissed very quickly.

(*a*) Copyists' slips are easily detected.

(*b*) If one reading makes the passage agree with some similar verse elsewhere and the other does not, the latter is probably correct, for the copyist might be tempted to make two passages agree, but not to make them differ.

(*c*) If words are missing from some of the early MSS. or versions, they almost certainly crept into the rest by insertion, and should be omitted.

(*d*) If one reading is harder to understand than the other, the harder one is likely to be correct, for the copyist would be tempted to simplify a hard passage, but not to make an easy passage difficult.

Grouping of MSS.—If none of these rules apply, we have to estimate the weight of the evidence for and against the reading in question. It will not do to assume that it is correct simply because it appears in the larger number of MSS., for many of these are copies from the older ones and must not be counted as independent witnesses: if fifty copies are made from a given MS., we have not fifty-one witnesses, but one. It is obvious that when a whole series of the same variants is found in a large number of copies they must all be derived from one ancestor, and it has been found possible in this way to group all our MSS. in four great "families," each representing a well-defined type of text. This process is not quite so simple as it sounds, for a copyist often referred to other MSS. besides the one he was copying, so that there is a certain amount of mixture of different types of texts or intermarriage between the families. Still, every MS. can be classed as belonging in the main to one or other of the families. It is not difficult to determine which are the four or five oldest and best MSS. in each family, and these only need be considered. The evidence is then arranged with one or more groups on one side and the rest on the other, and the two other kinds of witnesses are also called in to help us.

2. *The Early Versions*

The whole or part of the New Testament was translated into a number of languages at a very early date, and where the difference between two Greek readings is sufficiently great to make a difference in the translation, these versions are of great assistance. It is true that we only have the versions in copies, and the copies are generally not so old as our best Greek MSS. But if a translation was made say in A.D. 170, even though our copy of it only dates from A.D. 600, it shows us what reading the translators had before them *when they were at their work* in A.D. 170. The versions may therefore give evidence of very great value indeed.

The great versions were prepared for the Churches which spoke Latin, Syriac, Egyptian or Armenian. Several different versions were made in various dialects of these languages, and in course of time others also appeared as revisions of the earliest translations. Three are of special interest:

The Lewis Syriac. The best copy known of the first Syriac version is a palimpsest found by two ladies, Mrs. Lewis and Mrs. Gibson, at the same monastery in which Tischendorf discovered א. It contains about four-fifths of the Gospels, the remainder is lost.

The Old Latin. The first Latin version made exists in twenty-seven more or less complete copies. Many of them have suffered in copying and the variations are immense.

The Vulgate. Jerome, in A.D. 384–386, prepared a revised Latin version based on the original Greek and the existing Latin versions. This became the standard Latin Bible and is now the "authorised version" in use among Roman Catholics. The name "Vulgate" is given to it because it is meant for the use of the *vulgus*, or crowd, that is, for general or common use.

3. *Quotations by Early Writers*

Many ancient Christian writings have been preserved, and when they quote the New Testament, the writers show us what their copies of the New Testament gave as the reading *at the time they wrote*. They may thus carry us back almost as early as A.D. 100, very much earlier than any copy of the New Testament we possess. Their evidence varies in its value. Some of the quotations are made from memory, like those of a preacher, and they may be too loose and inexact to help us in finding the correct reading. Sometimes, however, the writer discusses the very point that is in dispute, or a commentator emphasizes the very word about which we are in doubt, and the quotation is then of the greatest possible value.

The Fathers.—The principal early Christian writers are known as the *Christian Fathers*. The names of the most important should be carefully learnt. The following list is abridged from that given in Pullan's *The Books of the New Testament*. The dates are only approximate, and in some cases are a few years earlier than those assigned by most authorities.

CLEMENT OF ROME. Bishop of Rome. *Epistle to Corinthians* .	A.D. 95
BARNABAS. Not Paul's companion. *Epistle of Barnabas* . . .	A.D. 95
DIDACHE, or *Teaching of the Twelve Apostles* . . .	A.D. 100–110
IGNATIUS. Bishop of Antioch and Martyr. 7 *Epistles* . . .	A.D. 110
POLYCARP. Bishop of Smyrna and Martyr. *Epistle to Philippians* .	A.D. 110
PAPIAS. Bishop. *Expositions of the Oracles of the Lord* . .	A.D. 130
HERMAS. *The Shepherd*, an allegory.	A.D. 140
JUSTIN MARTYR. Defences of Christianity . . .	A.D. 152–157
TATIAN. The *Dĭătĕssărōn*, a harmony of the Gospels .	A.D. 160–170
IRENÆUS. Bishop of Lyons. *Against Heresies* . . .	A.D. 185
CLEMENT OF ALEXANDRIA. Theologian	A.D. 190
TERTULLIAN. Carthage. Defences of Christianity	A.D. 200
ORIGEN. Alexandria. Great philosopher	A.D. 230

EUSEBIUS. Bishop of Cæsarea. Church History . . . A.D. 320
JEROME. Made a revised Latin version, the *Vulgate* . . A.D. 390
AUGUSTINE. Bishop of Hippo in North Africa. Great theologian. A.D. 410

G.—MODERN EDITIONS

Infinite pains have been spent, especially during the last century, on the minute examination of the MSS. and early Christian literature, and textual criticism has not become a very methodical and exact science. Of our oldest and best MSS. א was only discovered in 1844, and though B was catalogued in the Vatican Library in 1481, it was not "collated," i.e., carefully compared with other MSS., until 1669. There are therefore now great masses of evidence available that were not available when the Authorised Version was made in 1611. Hence the Revised Version is not only a more accurate and modern translation; it is the translation of a far purer text. Great editions of the Greek text have been issued by Lachmann, Tischendorf, Tregelles, and Westcott and Hort. The work has been so thoroughly done that there is now only a minute fraction of the whole concerning which there is any doubt, though the text of the Gospels still presents more problems than that of the Pauline Epistles. There are very few early writings in the case of which we can make so near an approach to the very words of the writers, and there is no doctrine of Christianity which depends for its support on a doubtful reading.

CHAPTER II

The Origin of the Gospel Story

A.—THE WORD "GOSPEL"

In announcing the birth of Jesus the angel said, "I bring you good tidings" (Luke ii. 10). Hence the story of Jesus and His message came to be known among the early Christians as the Good Tidings or Good News. The Greek word for this was *euaggelion*, pronounced eu-ang-gel-ion. This became in Latin *evangelium*, and so we get our word *evangel*, with the corresponding word *evangelist* for the writer of the story. But we have also a Saxon word dating from the early days of Christianity in Britain —*God-spell*, which probably means *God story*, though some say *good story*—and this has become our familiar word *Gospel*.

There is, of course, only *one* Gospel, the good news proclaimed by Jesus: what our four books give us is not four Gospels, but four records of the one Gospel "according to" four different writers.

B.—THE UNWRITTEN GOSPEL, OR ORAL TRADITION

Books were little used among the Jews, and their teaching was almost entirely oral. With the exception of Paul and John, the Apostles were not literary men: their special work was to preach, not to write. During the first generation there was little need for written Gospels: the story was passed on by word of mouth, and probably received a fairly fixed and definite form. This is called the *Oral Tradition*. But though the Churches founded by Paul knew the Gospel from his preaching, various difficulties arose in their Church life which had to be dealt with promptly, and as he could not go to them at the time, he had to write his letters. Hence we have the rather surprising fact that a large part of the New Testament was written before the earliest of the Gospels.

Contents.—We can form a fairly complete idea of the *contents of the Oral Gospel* by studying (1) the reports of sermons preached by Peter and Paul, e.g., Acts x. 34–43 and xix. 1–4, remembering, however, that these reports are very much abridged; (2) the references in the Epistles to what the readers had heard preached, e.g., 1 Cor. xv. 1–8. As the result we find that the Oral Gospel was very similar to our Gospel according to St. Mark.

C.—THE WRITTEN GOSPELS

Somewhere about the year A.D. 60 written Gospels began to appear. As many of these were very fanciful and erroneous, and the ranks of the Apostles were beginning to be thinned by death, it became important to record the true story of Jesus in writing before the eye-witnesses were all removed.

Apocryphal Gospels.—Luke tells us in his preface

(i. 1–4) that when he wrote a number of Gospels already existed in writing, and they continued to multiply afterwards. Some of the later ones survive and form what we call the *Apocryphal Gospels*. They are largely fictitious. They describe a boy who knew everything even as a baby; who worked ridiculous "miracles" that remind us of conjuring tricks, such as causing clay sparrows to fly; and who was a terror to all about Him: "No one durst anger Him, lest He should curse him and he should be maimed." Such "Gospels" show us the kind of legend that would be produced in the absence of sober histories of the life of Jesus.

The Four.—In marked contrast with the rest there are four Gospels which early and unbroken tradition connects very closely with the Apostles, and which are distinguished by their simplicity and sobriety. They were so soon recognized as the only reliable ones that between A.D. 140 and 170 Tatian compiled a harmony, or rather a combined narrative, from them, called the *Diatessaron* (literally, "through four"). Even earlier than this the four had become so established that we have fanciful reasons brought forward why there must in the nature of things be four Gospels and no more.

D.—THE TRUTH OF THE GOSPEL STORY

We shall consider later some of the reasons for believing that our Gospels date from a very early period and have behind them the authority of personal disciples of Jesus and eye-witnesses. But we may mention here certain reasons for believing that they give us the true story of His life, quite apart from any question as to their date or authorship.

1. *The narratives are sober, straightforward and matter-of-fact*, quite free from the romancing that we find in the Apocryphal Gospels. The Evangelists write with extraordinary calmness and moderation: even the story of the Trial and Death of Jesus is told without any trace of personal feeling, as if the writers were only concerned to state the facts fully and accurately.

2. *They describe a Jesus who worked miracles, but the miracles do not strike us as strange or incredible:* they are almost without exception works of mercy; they are always dignified; and they are in perfect harmony with all else that we are told of Jesus; in fact, they are just the kind of deeds that we might expect Him to do if He were the Son of God among men. "If the question be asked how it is possible to believe that any one ever fed five thousand persons with five loaves and two fishes, the answer is very simple: we are not asked to believe that 'any one' wrought so great a marvel, . . . the One of whom the statement is made is Christ, and it is just the fact that it is Christ's miracle that makes all the difference."—(*George Jackson*).

3. *They describe a character so beautiful, so consistent, so large and noble, that it must have been drawn from life.* Charles Reade, the novelist, has pointed out many little touches in the narrative which no writer of fiction would think of introducing. And it is incredible that the imagination of Galilæan peasants could produce a character so tender and

yet so strong, or picture a life so active and yet so sinless. It is equally incredible that they could produce teaching so sublime. If the story of Jesus and His teaching were fiction, it would require a man as unique as Jesus to be the author of such fiction.

CHAPTER III

THE SYNOPTIC GOSPELS AND THEIR CONNEXION

ANY reader of the New Testament must be struck with the fact that the first three Gospels give us very similar narratives. Reference Bibles, or, better still, tables of comparison, such as those provided in the Oxford *Helps* or Cambridge *Companion*, show us that, whilst there are very few parallels in John to what is found in Matthew, Mark and Luke, there are a great many close parallels between these three. They are therefore called the *Synoptic Gospels*, the name being derived from a Greek word which means that they look at the life of Jesus in the same way. Matter found in all three is called the *triple tradition*, or threefold story. Similarly, matter found in two only is a *double tradition*. Obviously, any pair of Gospels will furnish a double tradition. The longest and most important is that found in Matthew and Luke only.

A.—THE WRITERS OF THE SYNOPTIC GOSPELS

Except in the titles, these three Gospels give us no clue to their authors' names; but the titles certainly represent the universal belief of the Church at a very early date, and such evidence must count for a great deal.

The phrase "according to" is, however, a little ambiguous. It almost certainly means that Matthew, Mark and Luke were believed to be the actual writers; but it may perhaps mean that these Gospels were written by friends or disciples who followed the lines of their teaching.

1. *Authorship of Mark*

A very important statement concerning Mark is made by *Papias*, who wrote *Expositions of the Sayings of Jesus*, possibly as early as A.D. 125. As a youth he knew Aristion and John the Presbyter (or Elder), who had both been personal disciples of Jesus. He quotes the account which this John gave of the origin of Mark:—

> This also the Presbyter used to say: Mark, having become (*or* having been) the interpreter of Peter, wrote down accurately—not, however, in order—as many as he remembered of the things either spoken or done by Jesus.

As is shown on pp. 41, 42, there is a good deal in the Gospel to bear out this statement, and it is admitted almost without dispute that the second Gospel was written by Mark, and that it records the story of Jesus very much as Peter used to tell it.

2. *Authorship of Matthew*

Papias further makes a very interesting statement concerning Matthew:

> Matthew, however, wrote the *logia* in the Hebrew tongue, and every man interpreted them as he was able.

Two difficulties arise here:

1. Our Matthew is in Greek, and nothing is known of any earlier Hebrew form of it.

2. The ordinary meaning of the word *logia* is sayings or oracles, and it is insisted by some who take the word strictly that what Matthew wrote was a small volume containing the sayings of Jesus with little or no narrative.

Dr. Rendel Harris has, however, aroused considerable interest in a very early type of Christian literature known as *Testimonies*. These were collections of "proof-texts" and "prophecies" drawn from the Old Testament, and arranged for use in preaching Christianity to Jewish hearers. It is suggested that the *logia* Papias ascribed to Matthew were not sayings of Jesus, but a collection of these "Testimonies." In favour of this it may be urged that: (1) Fulfilment of prophecy in the life of Christ is more prominent in Matthew than in any other Gospel. (2) The "Testimonies" appear to have been grouped in "*five* books" and the Gospel of Matthew also consists of *five* great sections.

The opinion is fairly common, therefore, that Matthew did not write our Gospel, but a little book of the sayings of Jesus, or perhaps proof-texts or prophecies about Jesus, which some other writer used in compiling our Gospel. If this be so, it is "the Gospel according to St. Matthew" only in the lower meaning of the words "according to," that is, as following the lines of Matthew's teaching concerning Jesus.

On the other hand, up to his recent death there was still one scholar of front rank, Zahn, who maintained that Papias was referring to our first Gospel. He claimed that there are some indications that it *is* a translation from Hebrew or Aramaic into Greek. He also contended that it is straining Papias's statement to say that he meant strictly sayings and no narrative when he used the word *logia*. His view was, therefore, that the Apostle Matthew wrote the Gospel in Hebrew or Aramaic, and that some one else translated it into Greek, perhaps modifying it somewhat in the process.

Few, however, agree with Zahn in this. It will also be shown later (pp. 25–27) that the author of Matthew almost certainly used Mark in writing his Gospel. It seems unlikely that an Apostle would use the work of Mark, who was not one of the Twelve, as his chief authority in describing the Ministry of Jesus, which he himself had seen.

On the other hand, there are two facts that rather support the idea that Matthew was the author: (1) He was so inconspicuous among the Twelve that no one would be likely to think of him as the author of a Gospel, unless he were known to have written it. (2) In the list of the Twelve in Matt. x. 3 he is called "the publican"; in the other lists the disreputable occupation of his earlier days is not mentioned. But the one man who would not be able to forget his shame would be Matthew himself. These two facts, however, are hardly sufficient to build upon.

Hence it is best to regard the authorship of this Gospel as uncertain. Such a conclusion need not disturb us or lessen the value of the book. There is no question here of any false claim or forgery, for, except in the title, which is not really part of the Gospel, it makes no claim whatever to be by Matthew. Whoever the actual writer was, it remains just as true and just as much inspired as it would be if we knew who wrote it.

3. *Authorship of Luke*

If we compare the preface to Luke (i. 1–4) with the preface to Acts (i. 1), it is quite clear that the Gospel and Acts are by the same writer. He does not name himself in either book, but he claims to have been a companion of Paul in some of his travels and on his voyage to Rome. There are several indications that he was a Gentile, and some phrases in each book make it likely that he was a physician. Now, as is shown on p. 46, Paul in his Epistles mentions a man called Luke who was a physician and a Gentile, and who was with him in both the first and the second imprisonments at Rome. He is in every way the most likely of Paul's companions to be the author, and we may accept without any doubt the unbroken belief of the Church that he wrote both Luke and Acts.

B.—THE CONNEXION BETWEEN THE SYNOPTIC GOSPELS

There is obviously a close connexion between these three Gospels. The *Synoptic Problem* is the attempt to form a theory of their origin that will account for the striking resemblances and also for the striking differences that we find between them.

1. *The matter common to Matthew, Mark and Luke*

The Triple Tradition.—It is natural to begin by studying the threefold story, making Mark, the shortest of the three, our starting-point. A Harmony of the Gospels, in which the narratives are printed side by side, is a great help, but it pays to work out the comparison for oneself with merely a reference Bible.

Mark tells us nothing of the Birth and Early Life of Jesus, so that *the threefold story begins with the Baptism and ends with the Burial of Jesus.* If we take a penny copy of Mark and underline all that is found again in Matthew or Luke or both of them, we shall notice:

Remarkable resemblances. (*a*) The *narratives* are very similar. Almost the whole of Mark is recorded in either Matthew or Luke, so much so that the Churches at one time almost ceased to read it, for every copy of Mark we now have is descended from a single MS. in which the last leaf was missing (see pp. 44, 45).

(*b*) The *order* is very similar. When Matthew and Luke introduce additional matter, they generally return again to Mark's narrative at the point at which they left it. Further, Matthew and Luke never both desert Mark's order together.

(*c*) The *words* used are almost identical. Sometimes whole sentences are almost word for word the same. This will be clearly seen if three passages such as Mark ii. 3–12, Matt. ix. 2–8 and Luke v. 18–26 are written out in parallel columns, and the words occurring in all three are underlined.

Yet we also find:

Remarkable differences. (*a*) Neither Matthew nor Luke gives the whole of Mark's narrative, though between them they almost do so.

(*b*) Both Matthew and Luke sometimes change Mark's order, though not at the same points.

(*c*) Matthew and Luke sometimes use different words from Mark even when the meaning is the same.

Theories.—Many theories, some simple and others very complex, have been suggested to account for these resemblances and differences. The one point on which there is almost universal agreement is that Mark was the earliest of the three. The simplest and most probable theories are then as follows:

(*a*) *All three used the Oral Tradition*, which is supposed to have become almost as fixed as a Catechism in its wording and the order of its narrative.

Objections: (1) There is no evidence that the Oral Tradition ever became so fixed and precise as this. (2) The Oral Tradition originated in Palestine, and would be in Aramaic, the language commonly spoken there. The Evangelists would not be likely to hit upon the same Greek words so often, if each translated it independently.

(*b*) *All three used an earlier written Gospel*, which has now perished.

Objection: There is no trace of any such document.

(*c*) *Matthew and Luke used Mark.* This theory would account for the resemblances, and there is general consent that Mark was the earliest.

Objection: It is difficult to understand why Matthew and Luke should each omit considerable sections, though not the same sections, or why they should sometimes alter Mark's language.

Reply: (1) Both Matthew and Luke had valuable matter to add, and as their books must be short, they would be compelled to omit the parts of Mark that seemed to them less important. (2) They may have altered Mark's language here and there because they thought they could improve it; or because some form of the Oral Tradition was in their minds, and they preferred to follow that; or again because they were not copying Mark, but only using it as one authority, so that having read a paragraph, they would sometimes be able to compare it with other accounts before they wrote that section, and might thus forget Mark's exact words.

Conclusion: The Triple Tradition common to Matthew, Mark and Luke first appeared in Mark. Mark was used by Matthew and Luke, who omitted some portions to make room for other matter. They also altered it sometimes under the influence of the Oral Tradition with which they were familiar. The fact that they treated Mark with considerable freedom shows that they may be regarded as three witnesses and not simply one, for they did not repeat what they found in Mark like mere copyists.

This must not be taken as a final or universally accepted conclusion: it is merely a theory which accounts fairly well for the facts; but it will serve as a starting-point for further study of the subject in larger books.

2. *The matter common to Matthew and Luke only*

If we mark in Matthew and Luke all that appears to have been taken from Mark, there is still a large portion of each Gospel left. In this we once more find a great deal which is common to both, so that it is certain that Matthew and Luke had a *second source* in common. The fact that they sometimes agree word for word shows that this source must have been a written document and that it must have been in Greek. It consisted almost wholly of the Saviour's *teaching*, e.g., the Sermon on the Mount (Matt. v.–vii.) does not occur in Mark, but a large part of it is found in Luke vi. 20–49, and other fragments elsewhere, e.g., Luke xi. 1–4. Almost the only *narratives* are: (1) fuller accounts of the Baptism and Temptation of Jesus; (2) the healing of the Centurion's servant; (3) the message from John in prison.

This document is generally called "Q," from the first letter of the German word for "source"—*Quelle*.

Those who take the statement of Papias on p. 21 to mean that Matthew merely formed a little collection of the teaching of Jesus in Hebrew, generally suppose that this source Q, for which we are looking, was a Greek translation of Matthew's "Logia."

3. *The matter peculiar to each*

It has already been said that there is very little peculiar to Mark. But Matthew and Luke give us quite independent accounts of—(1) the Birth and Early Life of Jesus; (2) some parts of His Ministry; (3) the events which followed the Resurrection.

(*a*) *Special sources of Matthew.* Even those who deny that the Gospel as we have it was the work of the Apostle Matthew, admit that it owed a great deal to him, especially in its record of the teaching of Jesus. If the compiler was a companion or disciple of Matthew, some of the other matter peculiar to this Gospel may be the outcome of the Apostle's reminiscences and enquiries.

(*b*) *Special sources of Luke.* Luke tells us in his preface (i. 1–4) that he examined a number of existing narratives. As an intimate friend of Paul he would be able to draw on the Apostle's stores of information, and Dr. J. H. Moulton has shown that there is considerable probability that Paul was in Jerusalem at the time of the Crucifixion, and that Luke's account of the Passion describes many of the events as he saw them. There is also some slight reason to believe that Luke came into touch with the circle of women who accompanied Jesus, and some believe that his story of the Birth and Boyhood of Jesus may have been derived from Mary herself. Further, it is certain that as a companion of Paul he would make the acquaintance of many of the most prominent of the early disciples in Palestine, especially during Paul's two years' imprisonment at Cæsarea (Acts xxiv. 27), and he must have learnt much from them.

Summary of Results. There is still a great deal of uncertainty, but the sources of the Synoptic Gospels were probably as follows:

MARK. The Oral Tradition as taught by *Peter*.

MATTHEW. (Assuming that it was not written by the Apostle.)

1. Mark, modified by the Oral Tradition as taught by *Matthew*.

2. Q, which may be the same as Matthew's "Logia."

LUKE.

1. Mark, modified by the Oral Tradition as taught by *Paul.*
2. Q, which was possibly Matthew's "Logia."
3. Various early narratives (i. 1–4).
4. Information received from Paul's friends in Palestine and, perhaps, from the Virgin Mary and her circle.

4. *Recent Developments*

Two rather more complicated theories which have aroused much interest recently may also be briefly mentioned.

Streeter's Four-Document Theory. This supposes that a very early collection of material was made at each of the four principal centres of Christianity: Mark at Rome, Q at Antioch, one called M (the special source of Matthew) at Jerusalem, and one called L (the special source of Luke) at Cæsarea. Very important parts of L would be such parables as the Prodigal Son and the Good Samaritan. On this theory Matthew was compiled from Mark + Q + M, and Luke from Mark + Q + L.

The Proto-Luke Theory is that Luke compiled a first draft (*protos* = first) from Q and L. On the publication of Mark he enlarged this by adding narratives which he found in Mark and the Nativity stories which he had learned by personal enquiry from the circle of women, possibly from Mary herself. On this view Mark was not the framework with which Luke started, but the source of additional matter which he fitted into Proto-Luke.

CHAPTER IV

The Gospel according to St. Matthew

A.—The Life of the Apostle Matthew

Even if the Apostle Matthew did not actually write this Gospel as we have it, the unbroken tradition of his authorship makes it certain that it was closely connected with him.

Jesus found at Capernaum a tax-gatherer, who is called in Mark ii. 14, "Levi, the son of Alphæus." He may have been in the service of either the Roman Government or Herod Antipas. If he was under the Roman Government, he must have been a very half-hearted and unsatisfactory Jew. Jesus called him to follow Him (Matt. ix. 9). He gave a farewell feast to his old friends at which Jesus was present (Matt. ix. 10–13, Luke v. 29–32). At the same time he seems to have changed his name to Matthew ("the gift of God"). He is not mentioned again except in lists of the Twelve. Tradition says that after Pentecost he laboured in Palestine, preaching especially to Jews and writing for them in Hebrew or Aramaic. There are also vague traditions of missionary work later on in Ethiopia and even in India.

B.—THE DATE OF MATTHEW

It is very difficult to fix the date with any accuracy. Three dates are suggested:

(1) *Very early*, A.D. 43–50, the earliest of all the books of the New Testament. In favour of this it is said—(*a*) that Paul must have known the Sermon on the Mount when he wrote Rom. xii.; (*b*) that the Epistle of James is full of references to the Sermon on the Mount. But the parallels in Rom. xii. are not close enough to imply more than that general familiarity with the teaching of Jesus which Paul must certainly have had quite apart from Matthew. James, on the other hand, does seem to have known the Sermon on the Mount much as we have it. But it is not quite certain that this Epistle was written very early, and, even if it was, James may have used one of the documents which afterwards formed part of Matthew; whilst it must also be remembered that, though he did not believe until after the Resurrection, as one of the brethren of the Lord, James must certainly have heard *some* of the teaching of Jesus as it was uttered (see Mark iii. 31).

The great objection to a very early date is that, as we saw in the last chapter, Matthew almost certainly used Mark, and Mark can hardly have been written much before A.D. 60.

(2) *Shortly before the Fall of Jerusalem, which happened in* A.D. 70. If we are right in supposing that Matthew had Mark for one of its sources, it cannot be earlier than A.D. 60. On the other hand, it can hardly be later than A.D. 70, for, though such a passage as xxiv. 15–22 implies that the

great catastrophe was drawing very near, there is no sign that Jerusalem had fallen.

(3) *After the Fall of Jerusalem, about* A.D. 80. In this case we should expect to find indications that Jerusalem had fallen. There seem to be no good reasons in favour of so late a date.

Conclusion About A.D 69 seems a not unlikely date.

It is sometimes said that, because we "orthodox" Christians *wish* to prove that the Gospels were written early, our conclusions are prejudiced, and that they were really written much later. Harnack, one of the very greatest of Continental scholars and critics, certainly could not be accused of any "prejudice" in the matter, and his conclusions are a sufficient reply to such statements. He dated Mark, Luke and John even *earlier* than the most "orthodox" ventured to suggest, and Matthew he put within a year or two on either side of A.D. 70!

C.—THE READERS FOR WHOM MATTHEW WAS WRITTEN

The tradition that either this Gospel or one of its principal sources was originally written in Hebrew is not at all surprising, for it is unquestionably the story of Jesus for *Jewish readers*.

(1) The genealogy of Jesus is traced back to Abraham, not to Adam.

(2) There are continual references to Old Testament prophecies fulfilled in the life of Jesus.

(3) Emphasis is laid on the claim made by Jesus that He had not come to destroy the Mosaic Law, but to fulfil it (see v. 17–20).

(4) The Gospel is so arranged as to show the development of "the kingdom of God." This idea was specially interesting to Jews, as they had always professed to regard God as their real King, and the greatest of their kings as only His representatives.

D.—THE AIM OF MATTHEW

The writer is not merely a *historian* recording the facts, like Mark; he is also a *pleader* appealing for faith in Jesus. He endeavours to set forth the story in such a way as to remove Jewish prejudices and make it easier for Jews to believe in Him. Matthew is among the Gospels what Hebrews is among the Epistles, a plea that Jesus fulfils the Old Testament. The chief difference is that Matthew sets Him forth as the *Messiah* who fulfils the Old Testament *prophecies*, and Hebrews as the *High Priest* who completes the Old Testament *sacrifices* by His Sacrifice on Calvary.

E.—SPECIAL FEATURES OF STYLE

There are three distinguishing features in the style of this Gospel and the method of its arrangement:

(1) *The writer is specially interested in the fulfilment of prophecy.* See i. 22, ii. 6, 15, 17, 23, viii. 17, xii. 17, xiii. 35, xxi. 4. Some of the instances quoted are very striking, but one or two of them seem a little strange. For instance, in ii. 15 the words quoted from Hosea meant that God had brought the *nation* of Israel out of Egypt, and the

prophet was not referring to Christ at all. But the stay of Jesus in Egypt reminded the evangelist of Israel's stay there, and so he saw in their deliverance something that *corresponded* to Jesus' return from Egypt. If Jesus had never been taken to Egypt, no one would have imagined that a prophecy had been left unfulfilled; yet, when He did come out of Egypt, this devout student of the Old Testament felt that the deliverance of Israel *foreshadowed* His return from Egypt, and was a kind of *prophecy* of it. Commentaries should also be consulted on Matt ii. 18 and 23.

(2) *The writer is fond of massing the teaching of Jesus together with little reference to the time at which He uttered it.* Parts of Matt. v–vii. are assigned by Luke to other occasions, and some regard the great Sermon as a compilation from teaching uttered by Jesus at various times, see pp. 37, 38. In chapter xiii. he gives us a group of parables, though they do not all appear to have been spoken at the same time. Broadly speaking, he is more anxious to record the Saviour's teaching systematically than to give us exact details of the happenings.

There are five of these collections of the words of Jesus: (1) The life and character of the Christian (v.–vii); (2) the preaching work of the Apostles (x); (3) parables describing the Kingdom (xiii); (4) problems of life together in the Christian community (xviii.); (5) teaching concerning the End of the World and Judgment (xxiv., xxv.). Note that each of these collections is closed with almost exactly the same formula, "And it came to pass when Jesus had ended these words, etc." (vii. 28; xi. 1; xiii. 53; xix. 1; xxvi. 1).

(3) *The writer is fond of arranging his material artificially*, perhaps to help the memory. For instance, seven was the perfect number among the Jews, and so we find the genealogy (i. 1–16) arranged in three fourteens, and a cluster of seven parables in chapter xiii.

F.—MATTER RECORDED IN MATTHEW ONLY

We find here a large amount of matter not recorded elsewhere.

1. *Narrative*. In the story of the Birth of Jesus: (1) The visit of the Wise Men; (2) The massacre at Bethlehem; (3) The flight into Egypt.

2. *Ten Parables*. (1) The Tares, xiii. 24–30; (2) The Hid Treasure, xiii. 44; (3) The Pearl of Great Price, xiii. 45, 46; (4) The Draw-net, xiii. 47–50; (5) The Unmerciful Servant, xviii. 23–35; (6) The Labourers in the Vineyard, xx. 1–16; (7) The Two Sons, xxi. 28–32; (8) The Marriage Feast, xxii. 1–14; (9) The Ten Virgins, xxv. 1–13; (10) The Talents, xxv. 14–30.

3. *Two Miracles*. (1) The cure of the two blind men, ix. 27–31; (2) The coin in the fish's mouth, xvii. 24–27. [If the coin was found, this was a miracle of *knowledge* on Christ's part. Matthew, however, does not say that it *was* found, although in the case of every other miracle the evangelists always state that the result actually followed. It is possible, therefore, that this is not meant to be regarded as a miracle, and that it was only a playful way of suggesting to Peter that the small

coin required could easily be earned by catching a fish or two.]

G.—THE SERMON ON THE MOUNT

Comparison with Luke.—Probably no words ever written have exerted so great an influence upon mankind as Matt. v.–vii., the Sermon on the Mount.

There are considerable differences between the version found in Luke vi. 20–49 *and that given here.*

(1) Matthew's sermon was preached on a "mountain" (Matt. v. 1), Luke's on "a level place" (Luke vi. 17). The spot generally regarded as the scene of the sermon happens to be a level stretch between the two peaks of Kurn Hattîn, near Capernaum.

(2) As to the sermon itself—(*a*) Luke's is much shorter; (*b*) he gives us four Beatitudes and four Woes, as against Matthew's nine Beatitudes and no Woes.

(3) A good deal, including even the Lord's Prayer, is given by Luke in other settings. See Luke xi. 1–4.

It is, of course, possible that Luke is reporting a different sermon in which Jesus repeated some parts of the Sermon on the Mount; but it is also possible that Matthew may have included in the sermon some teaching delivered on other occasions. Many regard Matt. v.–vii. as a summary of the most distinctive teaching of Jesus rather than a single sermon. The facts of the life of Jesus having been well stated in Mark, the writer of this Gospel may have felt that a clear statement of Christ's message was needed before he went on to describe His active ministry.

Outline.—Whether it is a single sermon or a compilation from several sermons, it is arranged with great skill; indeed, the unity and symmetry are so perfect that many feel that it cannot be a compilation. On the other hand, the fact that Luke assigns the Lord's Prayer to another occasion is a serious difficulty, for it is almost inconceivable that Jesus taught the same prayer to the same disciples twice.

Subject: THE KINGDOM OF HEAVEN AND ITS CITIZENS

1. *The character of the Christian* (v. 1–9).

2. *The position of the Christian in the world* (v. 10–16).

(*a*) Persecuted by the wicked (v. 10–12).

(*b*) An influence for good, like salt that prevents corruption or a light that shines in darkness (v. 13–16).

3. *The Christian ideal compared with the Old Testament standard* (v. 17–48).

(*a*) It does not destroy the old, but perfects it (*vv.* 17–20).

(*b*) It is superior in its teaching about hatred, marriage, oaths, revenge, and neighbourly love (*vv.* 21–48).

4. *The Christian's temptations and dangers* (vi. 1–vii. 6).

(*a*) Religious display, e.g., in almsgiving, prayer and fasting (vi. 1–18).

(*b*) The love of money (vi. 19–24).

(*c*) Anxious care and distrust of God (vi. 25–34).

(*d*) Harsh judgment of others (vii. 1–5).

(*e*) The squandering of spiritual treasure (vii. 6).

5. *The Christian's resources in prayer* (vii. 7–11).

6. *The Christian's duty towards others* (vii. 12).

7. *The importance of being a Christian* (vii. 13–27).

(*a*) Some are unwilling to make the sacrifices required (*vv.* 13, 14).

(*b*) Some are hypocrites (*vv.* 15–23).

(*c*) Some hear, but do nothing (*vv.* 24–27).

CHAPTER V

The Gospel according to St. Mark

A.—THE LIFE OF ST. MARK

John Mark was the son of a certain Mary, who was apparently a prominent member of the Church at Jerusalem, seeing that Peter went to her house on his release from prison (Acts xii. 12–17). He was probably the "young man" who fled from the garden at the arrest of Jesus (Mark xiv. 51, 52).

Barnabas was either his uncle or his cousin (Col. iv. 10), and he and Saul (i.e., Paul) brought Mark from Jerusalem to Antioch (Acts xii. 25), and took him with them as their "minister," or attendant, on the First Missionary Journey (Acts xiii. 5). For some reason not stated he left them at Perga and made his way back to Jerusalem (Acts xiii. 13). Paul refused to take him on the Second Journey (Acts xv. 38), and in consequence Barnabas and Mark went together to Cyprus. There are traditions that Mark did missionary work in Egypt and founded the Church at Alexandria.

From Col. iv. 10, 11 and Philem. 24 we gather that there was a reconciliation with Paul, and that Mark was in Rome during Paul's first imprisonment there. During the second imprisonment

Paul asked Timothy to bring Mark with him to Rome (2 Tim. iv. 11). We may take it therefore that Mark was with Paul when the end came.

Turning now to 1 Peter v. 13, we read: "She that is in Babylon (i.e., the Church at Rome) . . . saluteth you; and so doth Mark my son." Mark was therefore intimately associated with Peter when he wrote this Epistle shortly before his martyrdom.

B.—MARK—A RECORD OF PETER'S TEACHING

The statement of Papias (see p. 21) that Mark was written as a record of Peter's teaching is confirmed by the fact just stated that Mark was Peter's intimate companion at the close of the Apostle's life. It is also confirmed by several *features of the Gospel that indicate that it was written under the influence of Peter.*

1. Some facts which might tend to glorify Peter are omitted, e.g.:

(*a*) His walking on the sea (Matt. xiv. 28–32).

(*b*) The great promise made to him by Jesus (Matt. xvi. 17–19).

2. Some facts rather humiliating to Peter are recorded more fully in Mark than elsewhere, e.g.:

(*a*) The stern rebuke of Jesus is uttered in the presence of the other disciples (viii. 33).

(*b*) Prominence is given to Peter's childish suggestion at the Transfiguration (ix. 5).

(*c*) It is remarked that at the time of Peter's denial the cock crew *twice* (xiv. 68, 72), and that he continued to deny his Lord even after the cock had crowed the first time.

3. Peter is sometimes named when the other Gospels do not mention him, e.g.:

(*a*) He drew attention to the withering of the fig tree (xi. 21).

(*b*) His sleeping in the Garden of Gethsemane was specially painful to Jesus (xiv. 37).

C.—DATE OF MARK

If we are right in supposing that Mark was used by Matthew and Luke, it must, of course, be dated earliest of the three. Assuming that it was written under Peter's influence, and that Mark's close association with Peter was at Rome, it can hardly be dated earlier than about A.D. 63. Some put it a year or two later. As both Matthew and Luke were probably written before the Fall of Jerusalem in A.D. 70, Mark must have been written some years before that date. But it is a notable fact that Harnack dated it even earlier than A.D. 63; he regarded it as *certain* that it was written before A.D. 60.

D.—THE READERS FOR WHOM MARK WAS WRITTEN

Gentiles.—There are several indications that *Mark was written for Gentile Christians.*

1. Jewish customs are explained, e.g., their ceremonial washings (vii. 3, 4) and the Preparation (xv. 42).

2. Aramaic words and names are translated, e.g.:

iii. 17: Boanerges, that is, Sons of thunder.

v. 41: Talitha cumi, which is, being interpreted, Damsel, I say unto thee, Arise.

vii. 34: Ephphatha, that is, Be opened.

x. 46: The son of Timæus, Bartimæus.

Roman Christians.—It also appears that it was written in the first instance for the *Christians of Rome*, who would be more familiar with Latin than with Greek. Facts such as the following are often quoted in evidence of this:

1. Some constructions are used that belong to Latin and not to Greek grammar.

2. A number of Latin words occur spelt in Greek letters, e.g., *speculator*, *denarius*, *quadrans*.

3. Greek terms which the readers might not know are explained by the corresponding Roman terms, e.g., in xii. 42 Mark explains that "two mites" were equal to the Roman *quadrans* or "farthing"; and in xv. 16 he explains that "the court" in Jerusalem corresponded to the Prætorium in Rome.

E.—SPECIAL FEATURES OF STYLE

Although this Gospel was almost lost to us, apparently because it was thought to be superfluous where Matthew and Luke were known, it is in some ways the most valuable of all, and we could ill afford to be without it.

1. *It is brief, but very compact*, so that it often includes details not found elsewhere, especially the exact names of persons and places, e.g., the playful name Boanerges (iii. 17); the name of the blind beggar, Bartimæus (x. 46); Alexander and Rufus, the names of the sons of Simon of Cyrene (xv. 21).

2. *It is particularly vivid and lifelike:* the narrative is full of movement and change, events succeeding each other very rapidly. The word "straightway" or "immediately" is in constant use.

3. *There are many references to the feelings and emotions of Jesus:* His anger (iii. 5); His surprise (vi. 6); His embracing the children (ix. 36, x. 16); His look of love (x. 21).

4. *The narrative is fresh and picturesque.* Compare the story of the healing of the demoniac boy, ix. 14–27, with that in Matt. xvii. 14–18 or Luke ix. 37–43, and note the additional touches supplied by Mark. Not the picturesque details in vi. 39, "the *green* grass," and in vi. 40, where "in ranks" means, literally, like flower-beds.

F.—MATTER PECULIAR TO MARK

This Gospel concerns itself only with the Ministry of Jesus, so that we miss the stories of the Birth and Early Life of Jesus found in Matthew and Luke.

The matter not recorded elsewhere consists of:

1. Two miracles: (1) The deaf and dumb man (vii. 31–37), and (2) The blind man at Bethsaida (viii. 22–26).

2. One parable: The seed growing secretly (iv. 26–29).

G.—THE CONCLUDING VERSES, XVI. 9–20

The most interesting problem connected with Mark has to do with its conclusion. It is almost certain that the last twelve verses do not belong to the original Gospel, and that the conclusion has been lost.

1. The two oldest MSS., ℵ and B, break off at verse 8, though it is inconceivable that the Gospel ended with the words "For they were afraid." The conclusion was also missing from the still

older MSS. from which the Lewis Syriac and Old Latin versions were made.

2. Verses 9–20 are very unlike the rest of the Gospel in style and phrasing. One Armenian MS. states that this passage was written by "Ariston the Presbyter," presumably because the original conclusion was missing. This Ariston was probably the Aristion mentioned on p. 21, a personal disciple of Jesus.

3. Some copies give quite a different and much shorter conclusion:

And they briefly reported to Peter and those with him all that had been told them. And after these things, even Jesus Himself sent out by means of them from the east even to the west the sacred and incorruptible proclamation of eternal salvation.

4. After *v.* 14 and before *v.* 15 the *Freer* MS., "W," inserts:

But they excused themselves, saying, This age of lawlessness and unbelief lies under the sway of Satan, who will not allow what lies under the unclean spirits to understand the truth and power of God; therefore, they said to Christ, Reveal your righteousness now. Christ answered them, The limit of years for Satan's power has now expired, but other terrors are at hand. I was delivered to death on behalf of sinners, that they might return to the truth and sin no more, that they might inherit that glory of righteousness which is spiritual and imperishable in heaven.

This rendering is given in Moffatt's *New Translation of the New Testament*. Before the discovery of W, it was known only from a quotation in the writings of Jerome. Moffatt regards it as being part of the conclusion with which we are familiar (*vv.* 9–20), but omitted at an early date.

CHAPTER VI

The Gospel according to St. Luke

A.—THE LIFE OF ST. LUKE

Luke and Acts.—As was said on p. 24, the two prefaces, Luke i. 1–4 and Acts i. 1, imply that Luke and Acts are by the same author, and that Acts is meant to be a continuation of the Gospel. The writer does not mention his name in either book, but there are large sections of Acts in which he uses the pronoun *we*, so that he claims to have been one of Paul's companions. (These are often called the "*We*-sections.")

Special touches in his descriptions of diseases, such as "a *great* fever" (iv. 38) and "*full* of leprosy" (v. 12) in the Gospel, and similar ones in Acts, indicate the interest of a medical man; and there is no reason to question the unbroken tradition that his name was Luke and that he was a physician.

Life of Luke.—In Col. iv. 14 Luke is called "the beloved physician." As Paul does not include him in Col. iv. 11, among "those who are of the circumcision," or Jews, he must have been a Gentile. He is said to have been born at Antioch in Syria. As there was a medical school at Paul's own city, Tarsus, not far away, it is not impossible that Luke received his medical training there; so that he may have made Paul's acquaintance in his student days. There is some reason to suppose that he was the brother of Titus.

Apparently Paul found him at Troas on the Second Missionary Journey, for *we* occurs for the first time when Paul sails from Troas to Europe after his vision of "the man of Macedonia" (Acts xvi. 10). [It is true that *we* occurs in Acts xiv. 22, but this does not necessarily imply that the writer was present then: it is probably merely the "we" a preacher uses when he unites himself with his hearers.]

Sir William Ramsay makes the interesting suggestion that the "man of Macedonia" was Luke himself, for his home at this time seems to have been at Philippi in Macedonia. Ramsay's idea is that Paul had been deeply impressed by meeting him in the streets of Troas during the day, and dreamed about him at night. It is clear that the man of the vision cannot have been just *any* man of Macedonia, for there was nothing in the dress or general appearance of the Macedonians to distinguish them from men of other parts. It must have been some one whom Paul recognized, and who he knew belonged to Macedonia; and there was no other man of Macedonia besides Luke whom Paul would be likely to know.

In any case Luke accompanied Paul, Silas and Timothy to Neapolis and Philippi (Acts xvi. 11, 12), and if not already a Christian became one then. The use of *we* ceases when Paul leaves Philippi after his imprisonment there (Acts xvii. 1) and it is not resumed until he passes through Philippi again six years later in returning from his Third Journey (Acts xx. 5, 6), so that he must have found Luke still there. This favours Ramsay's suggestion that Luke's home and "practice" were at Philippi, and it is quite possible that he had been at the head of the Church there during the interval. He now accompanied Paul to Jerusalem, and, eventually, on the voyage to Rome. He was with him during the first Roman imprisonment (Col. iv. 14 and Philemon 24), and also during the second Roman imprisonment (2 Tim. iv. 11), that is, until Paul's death.

B.—THE DATE OF LUKE

From Acts i. 1 it is clear that the Gospel was written before Acts, so that its date will depend upon that of Acts.

1. *Early date: before the death of Paul.* Acts concludes with the arrival of Paul in Rome, and makes no mention of his trial, release or death. Some argue, therefore, that it must have been written before Paul's death, say about A.D. 63, and that the Gospel must have been written still earlier, say A.D. 61, perhaps during the imprisonment at Cæsarea before the voyage to Rome (Acts xxiv. 27).

Harnack accepted this early date, and declared that it is now "established beyond question" that both Luke and Acts were written while Paul was still alive.

The difficulties are that:

(1) Luke tells us that many Gospels already existed when he wrote;

(2) Luke almost certainly used Mark, and Harnack's view that Mark was written early enough for Luke to use it in A.D. 61 still seems a little startling to most students.

2. *Later date: after the death of Paul.* Many do not admit that Acts must have been written before the death of Paul. Luke may have written the book later and yet have failed to mention Paul's death for one of two reasons:

(*a*) *He may have meant to write a third volume* telling of the death of Paul and the further spread of Christianity. This would make the somewhat abrupt ending of Acts more intelligible. Some argue that he must have planned a third volume because in Acts i. 1 he calls the Gospel "the *first* treatise," not the *former*, see R.V. margin. But there is little in this, for the Greeks of that time do not seem to have been any more accurate in this matter than we are, and we often speak of the "first" of *two* things.

(*b*) A better reason is that Acts is not meant to be a *biography of Paul*, but a *history of the spread of Christianity*. Luke was so little interested in Paul personally that he makes no reference whatever to his Epistles. But if his interest was in the spread of Christianity, Paul's arrival at Rome, the capital of the Empire, was the climax, and that is the natural stopping-place.

We are, therefore, not *obliged* to date these books before the death of Paul. The Gospel is assigned by many to the period A.D. 75–80. Some even profess to find signs that Luke was familiar with the writings of Josephus, which did not appear till

A.D. 93, so that they date the Gospel as late as A.D. 95. If Luke was considerably younger than Paul, he may have lived till the close of the century, but the evidence that he knew the works of Josephus is too slight to build upon with any confidence. It is even doubtful whether we can go later than A.D. 70, for though there are one or two little touches that may indicate that Jerusalem had fallen, we should expect Luke to have pointed out more clearly that the warnings of Jesus had been fulfilled if he wrote after the fall of the city.

Conclusion: We can only say that, like Matthew, Luke was written some time after the publication of Mark, and almost certainly before the Fall of Jerusalem, if not before the death of Paul.

C.—THE READERS FOR WHOM LUKE WAS WRITTEN

Theophilus.—Both the Gospel and Acts are dedicated to a certain Theophilus, see Luke i. 3 and Acts i. 1. He was apparently a distinguished Gentile convert. This does not mean, however, that he alone was expected to read them: he corresponded to the "patron" to whom literary men generally dedicated their works both in Rome and, until comparatively recently, in England.

Gentiles.—In its wider circulation the Gospel was intended for *Gentile Christians generally*, such as the members of the Churches founded by Paul. Note that:

1. Unlike Matthew, Luke makes few references to the Old Testament or to prophecies fulfilled in the life of Jesus.

2. He traces the genealogy of Jesus to Adam and to God, not to Abraham.

3. He substitutes Greek for Hebrew words, e.g., "Master" for "Rabbi," "lawyer" for "scribe," "verily" for "Amen," "Zealot" for "Cananæan."

4. He defines his dates in ii. 1, 2 and iii. 1, 2 by the names of Roman governors, as well as in the Jewish fashion.

D.—SPECIAL CHARACTERISTICS OF LUKE

Each of the Gospels has some distinctive features, and the special characteristics of Luke are so well marked that this Gospel is called by quite a number of descriptive titles, which have now come into fairly common use:

1. *The universal or "catholic" Gospel*, emphasizing the fact that Christ's salvation is for *all*. It seems as if Luke had caught the spirit of Paul, the great Apostle to the Gentiles. He makes frequent references to Christ's friendship with publicans and sinners. He alone tells of the conversion of Zacchæus and the Penitent Robber, and he alone records the parables of the Good Samaritan, the Prodigal Son, and the Pharisee and the Publican.

2. *The Gospel of Women.* He mentions many women, and always with sympathy, e.g., Elizabeth, the Virgin Mary, Anna, Mary Magdalene, Martha and Mary of Bethany, the woman that was a sinner, Susanna, Joanna, etc. Altogether this Gospel is marked by great *tenderness*: the failings of the disciples are dealt with more gently than in Mark, e.g., Luke seems deliberately to omit Mark's references to the ambitious request of James and

John, and the murmuring of the disciples at the costliness of the spikenard.

3. *The Gospel of the Poor.* Luke says, not "Blessed are the poor in spirit," but "Blessed are *ye poor*," and not "Blessed are they that hunger and thirst after righteousness," but "Blessed are *ye that hunger now*" (Luke vi. 20, 21). He alone gives the parable of the Rich Man and Lazarus, and he emphasizes Christ's warnings against riches. [It is an exaggeration, however, to say that Luke represents Jesus as teaching that money is evil in itself; he recognizes that money can be put to good uses, as it was by Zacchæus, the women who ministered to Jesus, and Joseph of Arimathæa.]

4. *The Gospel of Praise.* Apart from continual references to joy, we owe to Luke the Song of Mary or *Magnificat* (i. 46–55), the song of Zacharias or *Benedictus* (i. 68–79), the Song of the Angels or *Gloria in Excelsis* (ii. 14), and the Song of Simeon or *Nunc Dimittis* (ii. 29–32).

5. *The Gospel of Prayer.* Luke mentions some seven special occasions on which Jesus prayed, and he alone records two parables on Prayer—the Unrighteous Judge, and the Friend at Midnight.

6. *The Gospel of the Holy Spirit.* John, of course, records much teaching of Jesus on the Holy Spirit that is not found in any of the Synoptics. But Luke gives special prominence to the *working* of the Spirit: Matthew mentions Him five times, Mark four, but Luke fifty-four.

E.—THE AIM OF LUKE

If Matthew was written as an appeal to *Jews*,

and aimed at removing their prejudices against Christianity, Luke was written as an appeal to *the Roman Empire and its officials* at the time when persecution by the Government was beginning. Luke seeks to present Christianity as a Gospel for *all* mankind, a religion which the whole world should welcome, and of which no Government need be afraid.

F.—MATTER PECULIAR TO LUKE

Luke is singularly rich in narratives and parables not recorded elsewhere.

1. *Narratives.* (*a*) In the account of the Birth and Early Life of Jesus: the annunciation of the birth of John the Baptist; the annunciation to Mary; the birth and naming of John; the birth of Jesus in the stable; the visit of the Shepherds; the presentation in the Temple; the visit of the Boy Jesus to the Temple.

(*b*) The section ix. 51–xviii. 30 is largely peculiar to Luke.

(*c*) In the closing chapters the Conversion of the Penitent Robber and the Walk to Emmaus are specially interesting.

2. *Miracles.* Six are peculiar to Luke. (*a*) The miraculous draught of fishes (v. 4–11); (*b*) The raising of the widow's son at Nain (vii. 11–17); (*c*) The infirm woman (xiii. 11–17); (*d*) The man with the dropsy (xiv. 1–6); (*e*) The ten lepers (xvii. 11–19); (*f*) The healing of the ear of Malchus (xxii. 50, 51).

3. *Parables.* Eleven are peculiar to Luke, all important. (*a*) The Two Debtors (vii. 41–43);

(*b*) The Good Samaritan (x. 25–37); (*c*) The Friend at Midnight (xi. 5–8); (*d*) The Rich Fool (xii. 16–21); (*e*) The Barren Fig Tree (xiii. 6–9); (*f*) The Lost Piece of Silver (xv. 8–10); (*g*) The Prodigal Son (xv. 11–32); (*h*) The Unjust Steward (xvi. 1–13); (*i*) The Rich Man and Lazarus (xvi. 19–31); (*j*) The Unjust Judge (xviii. 1–8); (*k*) The Pharisee and the Publican (xviii. 10–14).

CHAPTER VII

THE GOSPEL ACCORDING TO ST. JOHN

UNTIL about a century ago there was probably no fact of which the Christian Church was more confident than that the fourth Gospel was written by John, the son of Zebedee, and that he was the "beloved disciple" often referred to, but never named, in its pages. But in the present day by far the most serious and the most difficult of the New Testament problems are those connected with the authorship and the reliability of this Gospel.

It will help us in our study of these questions if we remind ourselves of the main facts in the life of John as they are understood by those who regard him as the author.

A.—THE COMMONLY ACCEPTED STORY OF THE LIFE OF ST. JOHN

John was the younger brother of James and the son of Zebedee, a Galilæan fisherman of prosperous means. It is possible that Salome, the mother of James and John, was the sister of the Virgin Mary, and in that case John was the cousin of Jesus. John xviii. 15 tells us that he was known to the high priest and had some influence with his household. Unlikely as this seems in the case of a Galilæan fisherman, it should be remembered that there were many humble connexions of notable families, e.g., both Mary and Joseph appear to have been of the royal line, and somewhat later, when the Emperor Domitian enquired for representatives of David's line, there were brought before him grandsons of Jude the Lord's brother, working peasants, whom he dismissed as too insignificant to be any danger to the Empire.

John i. 35–40 implies that he was a disciple of John the Baptist, and first sought Jesus as the result of the Baptist's words concerning Him.

Later on Jesus called the two brothers to definite discipleship whilst they were mending their nets (Mark i. 19, 20). With Peter they formed a trio with whom Jesus seems to have been specially intimate, for they were present at the raising of the daughter of Jaïrus (Mark v. 37), and at the Transfiguration (Mark ix. 2), and they were near to Him during the Agony in Gethsemane (Mark xiv. 33).

The two brothers seem to have been of a warm and intolerant temper: they wished to call down fire on a Samaritan village which refused to receive Jesus (Luke ix. 54); and John rebuked a man who did not belong to their circle, but was casting out devils in Jesus' name (Mark ix. 38). Hence Jesus gave them the name of *Boanerges*, sons of thunder (Mark iii. 17). They were also ambitious, for they joined in their mother's request that they should be given the chief places in the Kingdom, and declared that they were willing to face any sacrifice for Christ's sake (Mark x. 35–40).

John occupied a place next to Jesus at the Last Supper, and leaned upon the Saviour's breast (John xiii. 25). After the arrest his acquaintance with the high priest secured admission into the court of the high priest for both Peter and himself (John xviii. 16). As He hung upon the Cross Jesus committed Mary to his care (John xix. 26). He and Peter were the first of the Twelve to hear of the Resurrection, and ran to the empty Tomb (John xx. 2). Later he saw the risen Lord in company with other disciples. At the lake-side Jesus uttered some strange words concerning him, which gave rise in his old age to the belief that he would not die, but survive until Christ's Coming (xxi. 23).

In Acts iii. 4, he was with Peter at the healing of the lame man, and was brought with him before the Sanhedrin. He also accompanied Peter on a visit to the new converts in Samaria (Acts viii. 14). Paul found him one of the pillars of the Church in Jerusalem at the time of the visit mentioned in Gal. ii. 1–10.

There are strong traditions to the effect that he was at one time banished to the island of Patmos, and wrote the Revelation there; that he afterwards settled at Ephesus, where he wrote the Epistles and Gospel; and that, after a very serene and beautiful old age, he died and was buried there.

Questions raised by this story

There are *three weak points* in this story, which bear directly on the question of the authorship of the Gospel, and should be noticed before we go further:

(1) It assumes that the "beloved disciple" was John.

(2) Acts does not mention John after chapter viii. 14, and some assert that he died early.

(3) Some believe that there was living in Ephesus about A.D. 90–100 another John, called "the Presbyter," or Elder, who had been a disciple of Jesus; and it is suggested that the traditions have confused one John with the other.

1. *Was John the "beloved disciple"?* It is shown on p. 66 that, if the beloved disciple was one of the Twelve, he must have been John. *It is conceivable, however, that this disciple was not one of the Twelve.* Such a conclusion would, of course, alter the whole story of the life of John, and imply that this "unknown" wrote the Gospel.

The most plausible suggestion is that the man who was afterwards known as John the Presbyter, belonged to an aristocratic priestly family in Jerusalem, and that as a lad of fifteen or sixteen he was a disciple of Jesus and a favourite with Him. It is argued that:

(*a*) Affection shown to a lad like this would be less likely to arouse jealousy than special favour shown to one of the Twelve.

(*b*) One with aristocratic connexions in Jerusalem would be more likely to have influence with the high priest than the Galilæan John.

(*c*) A well-educated lad would be more likely to appreciate the profounder teaching of Jesus than the comparatively illiterate Apostles.

(*d*) If his home was in Jerusalem, we can understand that the work of Jesus in Jerusalem and Judæa would bulk more largely in his Gospel than that in Galilee.

Reply. The theory is very attractive, and it has this great advantage over some others, that the writer of the Gospel would still be an *eye-witness*. But some of the arguments in favour of this view have little weight, and there are serious objections:

(*a*) Whatever the temptation to jealousy, Jesus *had* favourites among the Twelve, for the Synoptics show that He distinguished Peter, James and John from the rest.

(*b*) As stated on p. 56, it is perfectly possible that John may have had some slight connexion with the high priest, although he was a Galilæan fisherman.

(*c*) If Jesus had this boy disciple frequently with Him, the other Gospels would certainly have mentioned him. He would be too old to be the "little child" in Matt. xviii. 2.

(*d*) He would be too young to have a home of his own to which he could take Mary after the death of Jesus.

(*e*) It is almost incredible that he could write a Gospel and not mention John and James, who figure so prominently in the Synoptics.

2. *Was John martyred early?* This question is of great importance, because this Gospel was certainly written very late in the century, and chapter xxi. 23 implies that the writer, whoever he was, lived so long that the impression got abroad that he would not die.

Now James was put to death by Herod in A.D. 43 or 44 (Acts xii. 2), and Papias is reported by Philip of Side (Sī-dē), a fifth century writer, to have stated that *John also was put to death by the Jews*. This is a most astonishing statement, for Papias believed that John wrote the Gospel, which he cannot have done if he died early.

The great majority of English scholars hold that Papias has been wrongly reported, for Philip of Side was notorious for his inaccuracy. The reasons for refusing to accept his statement are as follows:

(*a*) If John was martyred *by the Jews* with James, or at any time within the period covered by Acts, Luke would certainly have mentioned it. Whatever Luke may have omitted, he would not have omitted this, for the attitude of the *Jews* towards Christianity was one of his main interests. His reason for failing to refer to John after chapter viii. 14 was not that John was dead, but that he did no strikingly original work in the world-wide spread of Christianity, which was Luke's supreme interest.

(*b*) Paul states in Gal. ii. 9 that he found John a pillar of the Church in Jerusalem. Most scholars hold that this visit to Jerusalem was the one referred to in Acts xv. 2, which took place some years *after* the death of James.

(*c*) There is nothing else in early literature to give the faintest hint that John died early, except the fact that some Churches later on observed the same "saint's day" for James and John. But this need not mean that they were supposed to have died together.

(*d*) There are very early and detailed traditions that John lived to be almost a hundred years old and died at Ephesus, and his tomb is still shown there.

3. *Is there confusion with John the Presbyter?* It is clear that a great deal depends on the traditions concerning the old age of John, and the consequences would be very serious if we had to admit that they might refer to the Presbyter and not to the Apostle. But this is not the case: the traditions recognize *two* Johns, and *two* tombs were shown at Ephesus. Papias in a list of early witnesses definitely *distinguishes* between the Presbyter and the Apostle. Further, Polycarp, whose testimony has been preserved to us by Irenæus, was himself a *disciple* of the aged Apostle *at* Ephesus.

Conclusions: We may wish that the New Testament had told us more of the later life of John, but:

(*a*) It is more difficult to believe that the beloved disciple was an outsider than that he was John.

(*b*) The persistent tradition that John died at an advanced age in Ephesus is too strong to be shaken.

We are now prepared to consider the question of the authorship more directly, with this fact fixed, that, *so far as we can tell, John lived long enough to be the author, and died at Ephesus, where this Gospel certainly originated.*

B.—EXTERNAL EVIDENCE AS TO THE AUTHOR

The testimony of early Christian writers is very

strong in favour of the Apostle John. It is quite certain that this Gospel was very soon recognized as one of "the four," and the evidence that it was regarded as the work of John is even stronger than that for the other three.

For.—Very interesting evidence that it was widely known and valued at an early date has been provided by the publication, as recently as 1935 and 1936, of two fragments of papyrus which are actually the oldest manuscripts known at all of any portion of the New Testament, for both of them are fragments of this Gospel. One shows that it was accepted (probably in Egypt) as an authoritative source, certainly before A.D. 150, and perhaps between A.D. 100 and 125. The other makes it certain that it was in circulation in Egypt before A.D. 130. Naturally neither fragment names John as the author—the Gospel itself does not do that—but it would be easy to bring forward many references to show that from the beginning this Gospel was associated with John. It is sometimes said, however, that none of these definitely and distinctly call him John the Apostle or John the son of Zebedee, and that the words used would apply equally well to any other disciple who happened to have the name John. But this fact supports the claim of the Apostle, for there was no other John so outstanding that the whole Church knew him simply as "John" without further description. Further, the testimony of Irenæus, Bishop of Lyons, really settles the matter. Irenæus was a disciple of Polycarp, who was himself *a disciple of the Apostle John.* Polycarp taught Irenæus that the Gospel was by the Apostle, and he at any rate cannot have confused him with any other John.

Against.—The evidence of any doubt on the matter in early days is almost insignificant. Marcion did not include the Gospel in his canon, but only because he disliked its doctrine, not because he doubted its authorship. About A.D. 360 a small sect, the Alogi, rejected it because of its teaching that Jesus was the Word of God, or *Logos*. They attempted to show that it could not have been written by an Apostle, but with little success.

We have the right to say, therefore, that *no belief concerning the New Testament was less questioned in the early days than that this Gospel was written by the Apostle*.

C.—THE TESTIMONY OF THE GOSPEL ITSELF TO ITS AUTHOR

Like the other three, the fourth Gospel does not name its author. But it suggests a great deal concerning him; and it has often been pointed out that if we read the Gospel, leaving out of consideration both the title and all the traditions, the narrative itself will lead us to the conclusion that John was the writer.

1. *The author was a Jew, not a Gentile*

(*a*) Some of the Old Testament *quotations* are taken directly from the Hebrew, not from the Septuagint or Greek version of the Old Testament, so that the author must have been able to read Hebrew.

(*b*) The writer was familiar with the *Jewish*

Festivals and the details of their observance. He even mentions the little-known Feast of the Dedication (x. 22), which was instituted in the time of the Maccabees to commemorate the re-dedication of the Temple after it had been profaned by Antiochus Epiphanes. There is, therefore, no reference to it in the Old Testament, and only one who was familiar with life in Palestine in our Saviour's day would know of it.

(*c*) The writer was familiar with *Jewish ideas*, e.g., their belief that the soul existed before birth, so that a man could sin before he was born (ix. 2). Similarly, he was well acquainted with their *expectations concerning the Messiah*, see i. 49, vi. 14, 15, and vii. 25–31.

(*d*) He knew their *customs* of purifying (ii. 6) and of embalming (xix. 39, 40), and their fear of ceremonial defilement (xviii. 28).

Objections.—There are two facts which have been brought forward to show that he was *not* a Jew, but they have little weight.

(*a*) He frequently speaks of "the Jews" as if he himself did not belong to them. But in these passages he is usually referring to the *unbelieving* Jews who opposed Jesus, though sometimes he means the men of *Judæa* as distinguished from the Galilæans. If he were a *Christian* Jew of *Galilee*, he would be quite free to use the phrase in these ways.

(*b*) He says in chapter xi. 49, 51 that "Caiaphas was high priest that year." It is argued that he supposed that the high priest was appointed for a year only, and not for life, and that no Jew could make such a mistake. But if we were to say that Victoria was Queen in the year of the Indian Mutiny, no one would take us to mean that the English sovereigns reign for one year only.

2. *The writer belonged to Palestine*

(*a*) He mentions a number of *obscure places*, such as Cana of Galilee, a Bethany beyond Jordan, and Ænon near to Salim; and exploration in Palestine has shown that he was correct in the names and situations of these places.

(*b*) He was well acquainted with the *city of Jerusalem*, e.g., he refers to the pool near the sheep-gate, the treasury, the pool of Siloam, and the spot called "the Pavement," with its Hebrew name "Gabbatha." It should be remembered that the destruction of Jerusalem produced great changes, so that only one who knew the city *before the year* A.D. 70 could be correct in such details.

3. *The writer was an eye-witness*

He *claims* to have been a direct eye-witness and asserts that he himself saw the blood and water issue from the side of Jesus: "And he that hath *seen* hath borne witness" (xix. 35). There is a great deal in the Gospel to confirm this claim:

(*a*) He mentions many *small details* which would only strike one who was actually present, e.g., *six* water-pots, five *barley* loaves, the *two* days at Sychar, the *two* days' delay after hearing of the illness of Lazarus, etc.

(*b*) He describes the *feelings* produced in those who saw and heard Jesus, e.g., the words of the men of Sychar after they had heard Jesus for themselves (iv. 42); the wish of the multitude to make Jesus king (vi. 15); the division of opinion concerning Him (vii. 11–13, 40–44).

4. *The writer was a close companion of Jesus*

(*a*) *The thoughts and feelings of the Twelve* are intimately described, e.g., chapter xi. 7–13.

(*b*) Long *private conversations* between Jesus and His disciples are recorded. Could any but one of the Twelve have heard the words of Jesus at the Last Supper recorded in chapters xiii–xvi, or His prayer for His disciples recorded in chapter xvii?

5. *The writer was John*

(*a*) There are many references to an *unnamed disciple* (i. 37 and 40, xviii. 15, xix. 26, xx. 2–8, xxi. 7, 20–24); and we are told that he leaned on the Saviour's breast at the Last Supper (xiii. 23). It is obvious that the writer is here referring to himself, but is too modest to mention his own name. Of the three who are described in the Synoptics as being particularly intimate with Jesus, the writer cannot have been Peter, for the beloved disciple is definitely distinguished from him in chapter xx. 2; he cannot have been James, for James was martyred far too early to have written this Gospel (Acts xii. 1, 2); he must have been *John*.

(*b*) Though they are prominent figures in the other Gospels *neither James nor John is ever named* here. The natural inference is that John himself was the writer, and did not care to mention either his own name or his brother's.

(*c*) In chapter i. 19, etc., John the Baptist is called simply John. If anyone but John were the writer, he would surely have distinguished the Baptist from the Apostle.

Conclusion: The Gospel itself indicates that the writer was either John the Apostle or some one who meant his readers to suppose that he was John.

D.—MODERN OBJECTIONS

The evidence in favour of the Apostle's authorship is so strong that it is surprising that it should be so widely questioned to-day. The two most weighty objections may be stated thus:

1. This Gospel differs so seriously from the Synoptics that it is urged that it cannot have proceeded from one of the Twelve.

2. The whole treatment is so profound and philosophical that it is said that a Galilæan fisherman could not have been the writer.

Objection i. The difference between John and the Synoptics

We have already seen that Matthew, Mark, and Luke give us very largely the same story. There are some points of disagreement, e.g., Matthew represents the centurion as coming to Jesus to ask for the healing of his servant, whilst Luke tells us that in his humility he made his request through Jewish friends; Matthew describes a certain miracle as consisting in the healing of two blind men, whilst Mark mentions only one. But such discrepancies are of little importance: they are no greater than the differences that we find in perfectly honest and careful biographical sketches of the same man.

When we turn to John, however, we find differences of quite another kind, that make us ask whether it can be the story of the same life, and be the work of an actual companion of Jesus.

(*a*) *The length of the Ministry.* If we had only the Synoptics it would seem that the Ministry of Jesus lasted one year or little more, but John's references to Jewish feasts imply that it lasted at least two and a half years.

Reply: The Synoptics give us few statements as to date, and do not commit us to one year. In Mark ii. 23 the ripe corn indicates the early summer, but in Mark vi. 39, "the green grass" shows that we have reached the spring of the next year, and there is still the remainder of the story to be allowed for.

(*b*) *The scene of the Ministry.* In the first three Gospels the Ministry seems to be confined to Galilee; in the fourth it is almost entirely confined to Jerusalem and Judæa.

Reply: (1) Though the Synoptics do not describe any work in Jerusalem before the Passion Week, *they indicate that Jesus had often preached there.*

(i) In Luke iv. 44 (R.V. *margin*) He is preaching in Judæa.

(ii) Scribes and Pharisees from Jerusalem would not have come down to Galilee to oppose Him, as described in Matt. xv. 1 and Luke v. 17, if He had never taught in Jerusalem.

(iii) The lament over Jerusalem (Matt. xxiii. 37) implies that He had *often* appealed to the city.

(iv) The general excitement at the time of His triumphal entry implies that Jesus was well known in Jerusalem.

(2) *John recognizes a Ministry in Galilee*, and does not really confine it to Jerusalem:

(i) He describes Jesus as belonging to Nazareth (i. 45).

(ii) He describes intervals spent in Galilee and important work there, e.g., the turning of the water into wine (ii. 1–11), the healing of the nobleman's son (iv. 43–54), and the feeding of the multitude (vi), all occurred on different visits to Galilee.

The fact is that the Ministry of Jesus alternated between Judæa and Galilee, and in the main the Synoptics describe the Galilæan and John the Judæan portions of it.

(*c*) *John's omission of important events*. John makes no reference to several of the most critical events: the Virgin Birth, the Baptism of Jesus, the Temptation, the Transfiguration, the institution of the Lord's Supper, and the Agony in the Garden.

Reply: If we are right in supposing that John was written long after Mark and Matthew, and probably long after Luke, there would be no need to mention events which had been fully described already, for the writer's object was to supply what was lacking in the other three, not to repeat their story.

Alleged contradiction.—On one very important

point there is what looks like an actual contradiction, for the Death of Jesus seems to be dated a day earlier in John than in the other three.

Reply: There is a good deal of evidence that the earlier date is correct, and a closer study of the Synoptics shows that they also favour it.

(*d*) *The difference in the teaching of Jesus.* There is a very striking difference between the teaching of Jesus as recorded in John and that found in the Synoptics. In the Synoptics we have brief, pithy parables; in John long discussions on much profounder themes. In the Synoptics we have short, clear sentences, with homely illustrations; in John long and elaborate arguments with symbols less easy to grasp, such as Light, Life, the Way, etc. According to the Synoptics the bulk of the teaching was devoted to the common people; according to John, Jesus seems to have spent His time in discussion with Jewish opponents and the training of the Twelve. There is thus a difference in *subjects*, *style*, and *audiences*.

Reply: Jesus had *three classes* to deal with—the common people, trained Scribes and Pharisees, and the Twelve. Naturally the subjects discussed and His mode of treating them would differ accordingly.

The Style of John.—Some feel that this raises a much more serious difficulty, for in this Gospel *the style seems to be the same throughout*: the words of Jesus, the arguments of His opponents, the comments of the writer, and the narrative of events are all given in the same kind of language. We cannot even be sure whether the great words, "For God so loved the world, etc." (iii. 16), were spoken by Jesus to Nicodemus, or whether they form part of the writer's comment which follows.

There are two considerations that will help us here:

(1) Jesus spoke in Aramaic, and His words had to be translated into Greek before our Gospels could be written. In the case of most of the teaching they record the Synoptic writers found this already done for them, so that there is a distinct difference between the language of their discourses and that of their narrative. But in the case of John the writer had to render the teaching into Greek for himself. Naturally he would use the words that came most readily to him, whether he was writing the narrative or translating the teaching; hence we find similar words and turns of expression throughout.

(2) The writer was an old man who had been meditating upon the teaching of Jesus for many years. It may be that with age the line grew faint which separated the teaching of Jesus from his meditations upon it, and that sometimes he gives us a paraphrase of the teaching in his own language, or a blend of teaching and interpretation. But there is also the possibility that, just as old people who read the Bible much and read little besides come to speak in Bible phraseology, John became so steeped in the words of Jesus that he could not escape from the style of Jesus even when he was writing narrative.

(*e*) *The difference in the portrait of Jesus.* Broadly speaking, the Synoptics represent Him as the Son of Man and Friend of Sinners, and *His Messiahship and Divinity are kept in the background*: He silences the devils when they testify to Him (Mark i. 34), and does not allow His disciples to proclaim that He is the Son of God (Mark ix. 9). In John, on the other hand, *His Messiahship and Divinity are prominent from the first*: at the outset the Baptist describes Him as the Son of God (John i. 34), and He acknowledges His Messiahship to Nicodemus (iii. 13) and the Woman of Samaria (iv. 25, 26). Further, He makes the most startling claims, such as, "Before Abraham was, I am" (viii. 58); "I and the Father are one" (x. 30); "I am the Way, the Truth, and the Life" (xiv. 6).

Reply: (1) *Though the Synoptics describe, in the main, the human Jesus, yet we also find in them the Divine Christ.* The Baptist's declaration, recorded in the Synoptics, that Jesus would baptize with the Holy Ghost and with fire (Luke iii. 16), is quite as remarkable as the declaration that He was the Lamb of God recorded in John. The Temptation story, with its repeated "If Thou be the Son of God," is recorded only in Matthew and Luke, and shows that the Synoptics knew that Jesus was conscious of His Divinity when His Ministry began. The Synoptics also record claims of Jesus quite as striking as any found in John, e.g., in Matt. xi. 28–30 He claims to be able to relieve all the woes of all mankind, and in Matt. vii. 22, 23 and xxv. 31 He claims to be men's final Judge.

(2) *Though John describes, in the main, the divine Christ, His real humanity is even more emphatically stated here than in the Synoptics.* Note such state-

ments as "The Word became *flesh*" (i. 14); "Jesus therefore *being wearied* with His journey" (iv. 6); "Jesus *wept*" (xi. 35); "There came out (of His side) *blood and water*" (xix. 34).

Conclusion: The differences between the fourth Gospel and the Synoptics do not make it impossible to believe that the Apostle was the writer.

(1) *The biographies do not conflict*: John supplements the Synoptics and dovetails into them. Where we can fairly compare them they agree remarkably closely, e.g., in the character of Jesus and the characters of Peter and other disciples.

(2) *The point of view is different*: the Synoptics describe the public work of Jesus, John His private life as known to His most intimate friend. The difference is not more striking than that between the Gladstone described in the newspapers and the Gladstone seen in his family letters.

Objection ii. The doctrine and philosophy of the Gospel

Doctrine.—It would be unreasonable to reject this Gospel merely because it represents Jesus as being the Son of God, for the other Gospels also describe a Christ who was divine. The Epistles of Paul, which were written between A.D. 50 and 67, make it clear that this belief had long been familiar to his Churches when he wrote; and the speeches in Acts show that it formed the central part of the Christian Gospel from the beginning.

Philosophy.—The real objection is not that John teaches the Divinity of Christ, but that it teaches the doctrine so philosophically. The writer takes hold of a term like *Logos*, or "the Word," which stood for a very complex idea in the philosophy of the day, and applies it to Jesus. It is argued that a Galilæan fisherman would be incapable of such profound thought.

Reply: Shakespeare was a very imperfectly educated village lad, Robert Burns was a ploughman, many great preachers have begun as colliers, and lads from the fishing villages and Highland glens have frequently distinguished themselves at the Scottish universities, especially in philosophy and theology. If John lived to a great age at Ephesus, a great centre of speculative thought, what right have we to say that he could not have become the dreamer-poet-philosopher who wrote this Gospel? And if he did live there, he must certainly have felt that there was room for a fourth Gospel, which would go more deeply into the life and teaching of Jesus, and set it forth more philosophically than the other three.

If it be said that John would be *too old* at this time for any such intellectual effort, it may be replied that Dr. Alfred Russel Wallace, who shared with Darwin the discovery of the theory of Evolution, was still writing on the profoundest subjects at the age of ninety.

Conclusions regarding the Authorship

(1) The Gospel was unquestionably written by an eye-witness.

(2) There is a great weight of early testimony in favour of the Apostle.

(3) The Gospel itself implies that the writer was either John or some one who meant his readers to suppose that he was John.

(4) The narrative does not conflict with the Synoptics in any such way as would make it impossible for an Apostle to have written it.

(5) In the light of other instances of remarkable intellectual development, it is perfectly possible that even a Galilæan fisherman might become the profound thinker who wrote this Gospel.

(6) No one else can be suggested as the author whom it would not be more difficult to accept than John.

Many of those who do not see their way to accept John as the author suggest that it is the work of a *disciple* or *group of disciples* of John, writing after his death *as his representatives*, and trying faithfully to set forth his preaching and to give his memories of the far-off days. Amongst other considerations they urge that such passages as xxi. 24 are editorial notes. Failing the personal authorship of John, this theory is open to less objection than any other.

E.—THE AIM AND CHARACTERISTICS OF JOHN

We can trace certain aims which John kept before himself, and which have produced the distinguishing features of this Gospel.

1. *To supplement the Synoptic story.* We owe to John the description of the *Ministry in Judæa*, but, what is vastly more important, we owe to him the description of the *private life of Jesus*. John's is thus the *most intimate* of the Gospels. It is difficult for

us to conceive how much the spiritual life of Christendom owes to the teaching of Jesus about the Comforter, the Bread of Life and the Vine; or how much easier it is for us to seek to live in communion with the unseen Christ because of His love for His disciples described in this Gospel. For this reason John's is also the *most spiritual* of the Gospels.

2. *To complete the portrait of Christ.* Matthew had represented Jesus as the Messiah, Mark as the Son of Man, Luke as the Saviour of the world. It remained for John to represent Him as *the Eternal Son of God.* It is true that we find the Divinity of Christ in the Synoptics, but they do not touch on the mystery of the Incarnation or try to conceive what He was before He came to earth—the *only-begotten* Son of God, the *eternal* Son of God. John makes us feel, as they do not, the immeasurable difference that there is between us and Him, a difference of nature that goes back to all eternity. Hence John's is the *profoundest and most theological* of the Gospels.

3. *To win men to faith in Christ.* John does not profess to be merely recording the life of Christ; he is an advocate pleading for faith in Him—

> These (things) are written *that ye may believe* that Jesus is the Christ, the son of God; and that believing ye may have life in His name (xx. 31).

Hence the narratives are not related in quite the same way in John as in the other Gospels. For John the events are not mere happenings in the life of Jesus, they are all *significant* of something deeper, and he is more interested in what they mean than in the events themselves. Even the miracles are not mere works of mercy, they are *signs* (see ii. 11, R.V., etc.), for they indicate the divine love and power that lay behind them. Thus in John even the history is made to teach theology.

Further, in this plea for belief in Christ, John selects and arranges his material very carefully. We find a clue to the whole thought of the Gospel in John i. 5, which may be translated thus: "And the Light is (still) shining in the darkness, and the darkness did not overcome it." That is to say, he wishes to set forth Christ as the Light manifested among men, and not quenched either by the opposition of men or by the tragedy of the Crucifixion. We may therefore say that John's is the *most philosophical of the Gospels*.

It may be very briefly outlined thus:

(*a*) The source of the Light (i. 1–14).

(*b*) The manifestation of the Light to the World (i. 15–iv. 54).

(*c*) The opposition of darkness (v.–xii.).

(*d*) The manifestation of the Light to the men of faith (xiii.–xvii.).

(*e*) The apparent triumph of darkness (xviii.–xix.).

(f) The victory of the Light (xx.).

(*g*) Conclusion (xxi.).

F.—THE TRUTH AND RELIABILITY OF JOHN

Even those who are confident that this Gospel was written by John feel that the question, Is the narrative literally true? needs to be considered.

1. *Did John mean to write history?* By far

the most dangerous attack that is being made on this Gospel to-day is the theory that it really does not matter who the author was, because, whoever he was, the book is a *subtle allegory*, and not a record of facts.

This important subject will be found rather fully treated in Peake's *Critical Introduction to the New Testament*, pp. 205–209.

The position taken up by those who hold this theory may be illustrated by the way in which they deal with the story of the woman of Samaria. According to them there was no such incident; the whole passage is only an ingenious allegory to describe what Christianity can do for a nation like the Samaritans. The woman of Samaria stands for the Samaritan people; her five previous husbands stand for the various heathen gods that they had worshipped in the past; her present illegitimate husband represents the fact that, though they were now wedded to Jehovah, they had no right to be so, because they were not of Hebrew blood, and so forth.

It is said that if we allegorize all the narratives, we shall escape the difficulty that John records incidents of which there is no trace in the Synoptics.

But, as Peake points out, the whole theory is far-fetched, for it is impossible to see what some of the narratives could be meant to represent as allegories. And even a story like that of the woman of Samaria is full of *very vivid and lifelike details*, which have *no meaning* as part of the allegory, and which the writer would not have introduced if he had been writing an allegory. Why speak of Jesus' weariness, why mention the place, the time, the well, the disciples' departure to buy bread, or their surprise when they found Jesus talking with the woman? If the woman is only a symbol for the Samaritans, what is the meaning of her running to tell the men?

Further, as we have already seen, the Gospel is full of small details of time and place, and all the characters, Nicodemus, the Woman of Samaria, the man born blind, Thomas, Peter, Caiaphas, and the rest, are so distinct that they must have been drawn from life.

Recent Opinion.—A very important feature of the study of this Gospel in recent years has been the growing sense of its value as history. As Professor Duncan puts it: "We no longer set aside its evidence as valueless when it happens to differ from the Synoptics." In some cases it *supplements* the Synoptic tradition, e.g., by describing a Judæan ministry and several visits to Jerusalem before the final one, which is the only one the Synoptics mention after Jesus' boyhood. In other cases it probably *corrects* the Synoptics, e.g., in dating the Last Supper on the Wednesday, instead of the Thursday, and the Crucifixion on the Thursday, instead of the Friday. Even the rather abstruse discourses given to the disciples and the controversies with the Jewish leaders are no longer regarded as out of keeping with the Synoptic portrait of Jesus. In addition to the two early fragments mentioned on p. 62, Professor Torrey's theory that all four Gospels were first written in Aramaic much earlier than has commonly been supposed, whilst it is not at all likely to be generally accepted, has created considerable interest, and has increased our confidence in their historic value, especially so in the case of the Fourth Gospel.

2. *Has the narrative been affected by John's great age?* Holding, as we do, that John wrote in old age, the question arises, Even supposing that he meant to write literal history, *can we be sure that he has remembered facts correctly?*

It has already been said on p. 71 that we must admit the possibility that with the lapse of time the words of Jesus may have lost something of their freshness and distinctness of outline, and that John may sometimes give us a paraphrase of our Lord's teaching, its spirit and substance rather than His actual words.

As regards events, an old man generally tends to forget the real *order*. A man of ninety will perhaps put some event that happened when he was twenty-five before one that happened when he was twenty-three. It would not be surprising if to some extent this was the case with John; and it would not really lessen the value of the Gospel.

But whilst there is no way in which we could *prove* that the memory of John was always perfect, the believing Christian will feel that, for him at any rate, that is not the end of the matter. Our own experience, and that of the whole Church, shows that the promises that Jesus made concerning the Comforter have been fulfilled: the Spirit *did* come, because we *know* that He is still in the world. Now one of the promises of Jesus concerning the Comforter was this: "He shall teach you all things, and bring to your remembrance all that I said unto you" (John xiv. 26). The other promises were fulfilled, and though we cannot *prove* it, we can venture to *believe* that this one was fulfilled also, and that the writers of the Gospels were aided by the Spirit in recording the words and deeds of Jesus.

G.—MATTER PECULIAR TO JOHN

Very little in John is recorded elsewhere. The most interesting and valuable of the records that we owe to this Gospel are as follows:

1. *Narratives.* (*a*) The first cleansing of the Temple (ii. 13–17); (*b*) The feet-washing (xiii. 2–20); (*c*) The appearance after the Resurrection when Thomas was present (xx. 26–29); (*d*) The appearance at the lake-side (xxi. 1–23).

2. *Miracles.* (*a*) Turning water into wine (ii. 1–11); (*b*) Cure of the nobleman's son (iv. 46–54); (*c*) Cure of the impotent man at the Pool of Bethesda (v. 1–9); (*d*) Opening of the eyes of the man born blind (ix. 1–12); (*e*) The raising of Lazarus (xi. 1–44).

3. *Parables.* (*a*) The Good Shepherd (x. 1–16); (*b*) The Vine (xv. 1–8).

4. *Interviews.* (*a*) With Nicodemus (iii. 1–15 or 16); (*b*) With the woman of Samaria (iv. 1–42); (*c*) With the Greeks (xii. 20–23).

5. *Discourses.* (*a*) The Bread of Life (vi. 22–65); (*b*) The discourses at the Last Supper, including the words of Jesus on the "many mansions," the Vine, and the Comforter (xiv.–xvi.), and His prayer for the disciples (xvii.).

H.—GENERAL CONCLUSIONS CONCERNING THE GOSPELS

The following table sums up the main conclusions at which we have arrived.

1. *Authorship.*

   Matthew, doubtful; *Mark*, by Mark; *Luke* by Luke; *John*, probably by John.

2. *The apostolic authority on which they rest.*

   Matthew, Matthew in part; *Mark*, Peter; *Luke*, Paul; *John*, John.

3. *The readers for whom they were written.*

   Matthew, for Jews; *Mark*, for the Christians of Rome; *Luke*, for the Gentile world; *John*, for the theologically-minded.

4. *Conception of Christ.*

   Matthew, the Messiah; *Mark*, the Son of Man; *Luke*, the Saviour of the world; *John*, the Eternal Son of God.

5. *Aim.*

   Matthew, an appeal to unbelieving Jews.

   Mark, a simple narrative.

   Luke, an appeal to the Roman Empire to abstain from persecution.

   John, a protest against faulty and defective views of Christ and an appeal for belief in Him.

6. *Date.*

   The dates most commonly accepted are: *Matthew*, A.D. 69; *Mark*, A.D. 60–64; *Luke*, probably A.D. 68 or 69; *John*, A.D. 90–95.

   The chief thing to note is that scholars now date the Gospels very much earlier than some of them did fifty or sixty years ago;

Baur's date for John was A.D. 170, Harnack's was A.D. 80–100. In fact, *Harnack's dates were even earlier than the familiar ones:*

Matthew, very near A.D. 70; *Mark*, before A.D. 60; *Luke*, before the death of Paul; *John*, A.D. 80–100.

This earlier dating, of course, implies that students are much more ready than some once were to admit that the Gospels are trustworthy and reliable.

CHAPTER VIII

The Acts of the Apostles

A.—AUTHORSHIP AND DATE

Luke and Acts.—Acts is indisputably by the author of Luke: both books are dedicated to Theophilus, the preface (Acts i. 1) states that one is the continuation of the other, and similar words and turns of expression are found in both.

Some have asserted that the whole of Acts is not by the same writer. But:

(1) The *plan* of the book is so simple and complete that it must be the work of one author.

(2) Even writers so unorthodox as Baur and Renan were convinced that it is a unity.

Date.—Acts must have been written shortly after the Gospel. Most scholars regard A.D. 70 to 80 as the latest possible date, whilst Harnack was convinced that both books were written before A.D. 64, which, according to him, was the year of Paul's death. Some few, however, maintain that Luke used the writings of Josephus, which did not appear till A.D. 93, and they accordingly date the Gospel about A.D. 95, and Acts still later. But the evidence for this is very slight and unconvincing (see next page).

Text.—It was mentioned on p. 7 that Codex

Bezae, or D, is remarkable for many additions to the narrative, especially in its text of Acts. Some of these passages read as if they were true, and they cannot be dismissed off-hand as late insertions of the copyist. Indeed, some scholars are so much impressed by the D text of Acts that they hold that Luke issued the book in *two editions*, the first rough, represented by D, the other more finished and a little abridged, represented by MSS. like א and B.

B.—THE SOURCES OF ACTS

It is not difficult to discover the main sources that Luke would be likely to use.

1. The *we*-sections and the bulk of xvi. 10–40 and xx. 6–xxviii. 31 would come from Luke's own *diary*.

2. As a close companion of Paul for many years he would learn the rest of the story of the Apostle from *Paul* himself.

3. *Philip the Deacon* was still living at Cæsarea (xxi. 8) during the two years of Paul's imprisonment there, and Luke would derive the early narratives from him and others who had been present at Pentecost, of whom there must have been many still surviving. It is quite likely that the letter of Claudius Lysias (xxiii. 26–30) was copied from the original, for it would be preserved among the Government records at Cæsarea.

4. The question remains, *Did Luke use Josephus?* Josephus was the Jewish historian whose book, "Jewish Antiquities," appeared in A.D. 94. If it could be shown that Luke used this book, Acts would, of course, have to be dated later than that.

The facts are merely that both writers mention the insurrections (Acts v. 36, 37) and the death of Herod (Acts xii. 20–23). But these were events which it was natural for both writers to mention quite independently of one another. So far from proving that Luke used Josephus, the evidence is rather to the contrary, for Luke's account differs a little from that of Josephus, as it would not have done if he had been using Josephus' book.

C.—THE PLAN OF ACTS

Title.—In Acts i. 1 Luke refers to his Gospel as the story of "all that Jesus *began* both to do and to teach." Acts tells us how the work of Jesus was continued after His Ascension by the Apostles. One book records the Acts of Jesus, the other the Acts of His Apostles.

Yet throughout the book the Risen Lord is regarded as *still working*: He pours forth the Spirit (ii. 33); it is His power that heals the lame man (iii. 16); it is He who gives repentance (v. 31); He appears to Saul, and He sends Ananias to open his eyes (ix. 17), and so forth. Hence the book might be more correctly entitled, *The further Acts of Jesus through His Apostles.*

A Story of Growth.—But Luke does not attempt to give us a complete history of all these "acts," or a complete biography of any of the workers. He selects among the narratives, and arranges his material in such a way as to show *the growth and development of Christianity.* But the growth of a Church may be of two kinds, *outward* growth or increase in numbers, and *inward* growth or development in character; and Acts is the story of the Church's growth in both these ways.

Subject 1.—*The Spread of Christianity*

Spread of the Church.—The words, "Ye shall be My witnesses both in Jerusalem, and in all Judæa, and Samaria, and into the uttermost parts of the earth" (i. 8), form a text for the whole book. The message of Acts is, in fact, the *Foreign Missionary Duty of the Church.* The book may be outlined thus:

Christianity and its Conquest of the World.—*Introduction:* The commission given to the Apostles, and their equipment to fulfil it through the gift of the Holy Spirit (i. 1–ii. 13).

(*a*) The Gospel in *Jerusalem* (ii. 14–vi. 7).
[Martyrdom of Stephen (vi. 8–viii. 1).]
(*b*) The Gospel in *Judæa* and *Samaria* (viii.).
(*c*) The Gospel in *Syria* (ix.–xi.).
[Persecution in Jerusalem (xii.).]
(*d*) The Gospel in *Asia Minor* through Paul's First Journey (xiii., xiv.).
[The Council at Jerusalem (xv. 1–35).]
(*e*) The Gospel in *Europe* through Paul's Second and Third Journeys (xv. 36–xxi. 16).
[The arrest of Paul and his imprisonment at Cæsarea (xxi. 17–xxvi. 32).]
[Paul's voyage to Rome (xxvii. 1–xxviii. 15).]
(*f*) The Gospel at *Rome* (xxviii. 16–31).

Luke's interest is not in the Churches or in the persons mentioned, but in the *progress* of the Gospel. He says little about work in Palestine after the

Church is founded in Asia Minor, and little about most of the Churches in Asia Minor after Europe has been entered. In the same way he drops Peter out of the story as soon as his distinctly pioneer work is ended. He omits from the story of Paul most of the events referred to in 2 Cor. xi. 24–27, and makes no mention of his Epistles; and when Paul is settled in Rome, he tells us nothing of what happened to him afterwards—the Gospel has reached Rome, and that is the climax of the book.

Subject 2.—The internal development of the Church

Internal Development.—Acts is also the story of the growth of the Church in the second way: Luke shows us how it developed in its belief and organization.

Christianity in its Infancy and Youth.—1. *The development of the spirit of brotherhood.* (*a*) Simple-hearted sharing of goods. (*b*) More systematic care for the poor members by the appointment of Deacons. (*c*) Contributions from Paul's Gentile Churches for the poor Christians of Jerusalem.

2. *The development of Christian character.* (*a*) The Church purged of hypocrites like Ananias and Sapphira. (*b*) The Church refined by the fire of successive persecutions.

3. *The development of the missionary spirit.* (1) Jews and *strict* proselytes only admitted. (*b*) Cornelius, an *uncircumcised* proselyte, admitted (x.). (*c*) Converts direct from heathenism freely admitted without any submission to the Jewish law (xv.).

4. *The development of doctrine.* The view of

Jesus as the Son of God gradually becomes clearer. The names used at different points show the advance: (*a*) "Jesus of Nazareth"; (*b*) "Jesus the Christ," i.e., Jesus who is the Messiah; (*c*) "Jesus Christ of Nazareth"; (*d*) "Jesus Christ" as a definite proper name.

5. *The development in organization.* (*a*) Apostles the only officials. (*b*) Appointment of Deacons. (*c*) Appointment of Elders or Presbyters.

6. *The development in freedom of worship.* (*a*) The Christians of Jerusalem still use the Temple and observe the Jewish hours of prayer, etc. (*b*) Before the close of the book the Gentile Churches are quite independent of the Temple or the synagogues, though Jewish Christians still observe the Jewish festivals if they wish to do so.

D.—THE MINUTE ACCURACY OF ACTS

Few question the substantial truth of the travel stories in the second half of Acts, but it is surprising to find how extremely accurate Luke has proved to be in many of the small details. Sir William Ramsay spent a large part of his life in the exploration of Asia Minor. He started as a young man with the belief that Acts was the most fanciful and the least reliable of the books that tell us anything of Asia Minor at that period. His researches among the ruins of ancient cities, monuments, inscriptions, and coins, led him to the conclusion that Acts is quite extraordinarily accurate.

(1) *Geography.*—Luke is correct in his references to *geographical boundaries, etc.* Few intelligent Englishmen on a walking tour through England

would be able to say to which counties some of the smaller places on their rout belong. But Luke states quite correctly that Lystra and Derbe were cities of Lycaonia, and that Iconium was not.

(2) *Official Titles.—The titles of provincial governors and of city magistrates* varied greatly at different *periods* and in different *localities*. Some cities were "free," some were Roman "colonies," and in other cases the form of government had special features. Yet coins and inscriptions show that, for the period to which he refers, Luke was always correct in his titles, e.g., Cyprus had not always a "proconsul," but Luke was quite right in saying that it had one at the time of Paul's visit (xiii. 8). In the same way the R.V. or its margin shows that he speaks of "prætors" attended by "lictors" at Philippi (xvi. 20, 35), "politarchs" or "rulers of the city" at Thessalonica (xvii. 6), "Asiarchs" at Ephesus (xix. 31); and in all these instances his statement is strictly correct. Similarly, it should be noted that at Philippi, which was a Roman "colony," Paul and Silas would be "beaten with rods" in the Roman fashion, as Luke states (Acts xvi. 22, R.V.), and not scourged with whips in the Jewish fashion.

In the case of the Gospel there is still debate and uncertainty concerning Luke's reference to Quirinius (or Cyrenius) as governor of Syria in the year of Jesus' birth (Luke ii. 2). It is certain that he was governor in A.D. 6, but if Jesus was born in the year we call 8 B.C., as seems most likely, there is no satisfying evidence that Quirinius was in office then. On the other hand, research confirms Luke's statement in iii. 1 that Lysanias *was* tetrarch of Abilene about the time referred to there.

The most interesting newer evidence is that bearing upon the *census*. Actual census papers have been unearthed which show that there was a census of the Roman Empire every fourteen years, in A.D. 6, A.D. 20, A.D. 34, etc. One would be due to fall in 8 B.C. No census papers for this have been found as yet, but it is quite possible that they may be discovered any day. Such census papers, however, as have come to light make it clear that every man was required to register himself "in his own city," however inconvenient it might be to return there, thus confirming the explanation Luke gives of the visit of Joseph and Mary to Bethlehem.

(3) *Voyage to Rome.*—The details of *the voyage to Rome* are extraordinarily minute and accurate, the more so when we consider how difficult it is for a landsman to use nautical terms correctly.

E.—THE TRUTH OF THE EARLY NARRATIVES IN ACTS

Whilst few question the reliability of the second half of Acts, some throw doubt on the earlier parts of the narrative, on the ground that Luke had to depend here on information supplied by others.

It must be remembered, however, that he would have opportunities of questioning witnesses of the highest character, like Philip the Deacon, who had never left Palestine. Further, the speeches of Peter in these early chapters show several points of resemblance with the style of 1 Peter, and witnesses who could preserve Peter's turns of speech correctly would not be likely to err in their recollection of the facts.

But our belief in these early narratives is specially confirmed by *the natural way in which Luke has reproduced the feelings and ideas of those first days of Christianity*.

1.—*Early Ideas*. It is clear that after Pentecost the disciples would still have to shake off their narrow Jewish ideas, and accustom themselves to Christian ways of thinking. Now Luke was a Gentile, and had never held these Jewish ideas, and the Christianity he knew was later and was free from them. Yet note *how perfectly he represents the confused thought of the first days:*

(*a*) The different names used for Jesus show that they had not yet got used to thinking of Him as the very Son of God.

(*b*) They had hardly grasped as yet the idea of salvation for all: Jesus is to give repentance to *Israel* (v. 31), and He is sent to the Jews *first* (iii. 26).

(*c*) They still clung to the Temple and observed the "prayers," i.e., the Jewish hours of prayer, just as the first Methodists continued to attend the Parish Church in addition to their own services.

2.—*Early Opposition. Luke appears to describe exactly the character of the early opposition to Christianity:* he tells us that at first only the Sadducees opposed it, but that when the Gospel began to be preached to the Gentiles the Pharisees joined in the persecution. Now, when Luke came to Palestine one section was as bitter as the other. Yet the statement of these early chapters quite agrees with the character of the two parties. The Sadducees were worldly-minded men, intensely anxious to keep on good terms with the Roman Government. They regarded Christianity as a dsiturbing influence that would produce trouble with their rulers; that is, they opposed it on *political* grounds. The Pharisees hated the Roman Government, and would have been glad to see Christianity or anything else produce a successful revolution. But when the Gospel was sent to the Gentiles, it was no longer a political question, but a *religious* one; their Jewish pride and bigotry were roused, and they, too, joined in the persecution.

There was nothing in Luke's own experience that would have enabled him to represent those early days so naturally; he must have had informants who were able to recall them very accurately. We are therefore warranted in taking his general narrative as true.

F.—THE COUNCIL OF JERUSALEM

Circumcision controversy.—Before leaving Acts we must notice what was by far the greatest controversy of the first generation of Christianity.

The first Christians were either Jews or full proselytes, i.e., Gentiles who had been circumcised and who accepted the whole Jewish system. At first they took it for granted that *every Christian* would also be a *Jew*. But presently, to the intense surprise of Peter and the rest, the Holy Ghost was given to Cornelius, who was *not* circumcised. Before long converts from heathenism began to multiply, and the Church was faced with a very serious problem: *Could a man be a Christian without being circumcised?* or in other words, *Could a man become a Christian without becoming a Jew?*

To us it presents no difficulty, but many of those who had been brought up as Jews could not see that Jewish observances no longer had any meaning, and that Christ saves us, not by faith plus circumcision, but by faith alone. Those who insisted that heathen converts must be circumcised were called *Judaists*. The controversy became exceedingly bitter, and lasted many years.

The first attempt to settle the question is described in Acts xv. No Church Council has ever had any more momentous decision to make than this *Council of Jerusalem*, for the whole future of Christianity was at stake: if the Judaists had triumphed, Christianity would have become a little Jewish sect, and not a religion for the whole world. The decision, quoted in chapter xv. 28, 29, was in part a compromise, but on the main question the verdict was clear: *Gentile Christians need not be circumcised.*

The Judaists v. Paul.—But that did not really end the controversy. Paul, as the most thoroughgoing champion of freedom for the Gentiles, was all his life attacked by the Judaists. They visited his Churches, stirring up suspicion against him, denying that he was really an Apostle, and trying to persuade his converts to be circumcised. The bulk of the Churches of Galatia went over to the enemy, and the Epistle to the Galatians was an indignant protest and a pathetic appeal to them to return to the Gospel of salvation by simple faith in

Christ. We also find traces of the struggle in several other Epistles. But in course of time the Gentile Christians became far more numerous than the Jewish, and the controversy died a natural death, for the simple reason that Jews ceased to become Christians, and the nation as a whole rejected Christianity, as it does still.

CHAPTER IX

The Life and Writings of St. Paul

Before we proceed to the study of the Epistles in detail, there are several important subjects to be considered that concern them as a group.

A.—THE PROMINENCE OF LETTERS IN THE NEW TESTAMENT

The Epistles.—It is one of the surprises of the New Testament that it consists very largely of letters. We can quite well understand that a missionary like Paul would be obliged to write to his Churches if difficulties arose and he was unable to visit them. We can understand, too, that, as he was on affectionate terms with most of his Churches, his communication would generally be as free and informal as possible. These letters would, of course, be read in the Churches to which they were addressed. The surprising thing is that within a comparatively short time they were also read in other Churches, and before long came to be classed as *Scripture*.

Human documents.—If we were to try to imagine what form a written revelation from God would be likely to take, the letter is almost the last form of composition of which we should think, for letters are intensely *human* documents, coloured by the personality of the writer and by that of the reader too. Yet of the twenty-seven books of the New Testament no less than twenty-one are letters, thirteen of them claiming to be by Paul. Most of them are very like our own letters: they open and close with personal greetings, some of them are saturated with the affection of the Apostle for his readers, and they were almost all written because of some passing circumstance in his life or theirs. Who would have imagined that part of God's revelation would be enshrined in a short letter written to a gentleman about his runaway slave?

Yet we have surely little reason to be surprised that in the Bible divine truth comes to us embedded in human documents. The belief that distinguishes Christianity from all other religions is that in Jesus Christ *the divine and the human were combined*, and we also believe that it is *because* He is Man as well as God that He is fitted to be our Saviour. May it not be that the Bible is a more effective revelation of God to us because it includes so many human elements? These human elements produce some difficulties and apparent inconsistencies, yet they bring the Bible nearer to us; and probably God's message reaches our hearts more effectually in this way than if the Bible had been an entirely divine book, coming down from Heaven without possibility of human error or defect.

B.—THE STRUCTURE OF THE EPISTLES

General Outline.—The Epistles are arranged in much the same way as ordinary letters of the period, a specimen of which may be seen in the letter of

Claudius Lysias to Felix (Acts xxiii. 26–30). The general outline is as follows:

1. *Salutation.* Paul takes the common Greek formula, "So-and-so to So-and-So, greeting," and Christianizes it by substituting for the word "greeting," such beautiful Christian terms as "grace," "mercy," and "peace."

2. *Thanksgiving* to God for the good that he knows of his readers. (In Galatians there is no thanksgiving, for they had lapsed grievously.)

3. *Prayer* for their further progress.

4. Any *news* that may interest them.

5. *Discussion of the doctrines or difficulties* that led to the writing of the Epistle. (This forms the main body of the letter.)

6. *Practical exhortations and encouragements*, mostly suggested by the doctrine discussed.

7. *Greetings* to various friends, corresponding to our "Give my kind regards (or love) to So-and-So."

8. *Benediction.* Paul Christianizes the formal "Farewell" of the everyday Greek letter by substituting a beautiful Christian wish.

C.—SOME ADVANTAGES OF THE LETTER FORM

It will readily be seen that in several ways these letters are more helpful to us than if Paul had written formal treatises on doctrine, because they include many *chance references* to himself and to others, which are of great interest and value.

1. *They deal with the practical difficulties and perils of the Christian life.* They were written as they were

needed, and because they were needed, and the needs of the Church to-day are very much the same as they were then. There is still party spirit in some Churches, as there was at Corinth; ritualism is still a snare, as it was among the Galatians; speculation may still lead us into doctrinal error, as it did the Colossians; masters and servants still need to be reminded of their proper relation to one another as Christians, like Philemon and his slave Onesimus. These Epistles interest and help us, because they deal with needs and difficulties which actually arose, and deal with them simply and directly.

2. *These letters show us the very heart of the writer.* We know Cowper far better from his letters than from his poems; and we reach the heart of Gladstone, not in his speeches, but in his correspondence with his family and friends. Similarly, in his Epistles Paul *reveals himself*, his sense of sin, his aspirations after holiness, his love for souls, and his utter abandonment to Christ. What a passion of love for unbelieving Israel is expressed in the words "I could wish that I myself were anathema (*accursed*) from Christ for my brethren's sake" (Rom. ix. 3); and what pathetic regret for the wasted years in the words "Who also have been in Christ *before* me!" (Rom. xvi. 7). Could any elaborate statement express so vividly how much he found in Christ, and how sure his hope of the future was, as the simple words, "For to me to live is Christ, and to die is gain" (Phil. i. 21)?

Such glimpses of the inner life of the greatest and most heroic of Christ's followers are hardly less precious than the Gospel story itself. In some ways Paul's example is even more directly helpful than that of Jesus; it shows us what a Christian can be, and we are not called to be Christs, but Christians.

3. *The Epistles throw light on the character of the Churches:* we see them as they appeared to one who knew them from within; we see them with all their excellences, but also with all their defects. Every difficulty Paul deals with and every sin he denounces shows us that the progress of Christianity has always been slow, that the Church has never been ideally perfect, and that the Christian worker has always experienced some disappointments.

4. *The Epistles show us clearly what were the central and most deeply rooted beliefs of the earliest Christians.* It is admitted, practically without dispute, that at least the four great Epistles, Romans, 1 and 2 Corinthians, and Galatians, were written by Paul, and written within about twenty-five years of the Crucifixion. But we find that in these Epistles such doctrines as the Divinity of Christ and Atonement by His Death are spoken of as if the readers had been familiar with them ever since they became Christians, whilst Paul refers to the Resurrection of Jesus as naturally as we refer to the death of King George V. Yet at this time they were still multitudes living *who had seen Jesus for themselves.* Hence the Epistles are one great pillar of the Christian Faith: they show (1) that these beliefs were not the creation of men's fancy two or three generations after Christ's Death; and (2) that those who had seen the life of Jesus on earth did not find it impossible to believe that He

was the very Son of God and the Redeemer of the world.

D.—THE AIM OF THE EPISTLES

So far we have considered ways in which the Epistles are valuable to us by their *incidental references* to the writer and his readers, and to their beliefs. But we have still to consider the *direct aim* that Paul had in writing them. This will need to be dealt with in detail as we study the various Epistles. But taking them as a whole, we may say that Paul achieved two great results; and it is because of these that the Epistles form part of the great revelation of God and are included in our Bibles.

1. *He sought to explain the great Christian doctrines.* He had no need to teach the Romans that the Death of Christ saves us, but there was need to explain *how* it does so; Paul does not give us a *proof* of the Atonement, but he does give us a *theory* of it. Similarly, there was no need to prove to most of the Corinthians that there will be a resurrection of the dead, but it was a great thing that Paul should explain what form that resurrection will take.

2. *Paul applied the great Christian doctrines to daily life.* Christianity is not simply a belief: it is a new kind of life inspired by that belief. It is often said that theology is unpractical; and there is a good deal of cant expressed in catch-phrases, such as "Not creeds, but deeds." Paul shows that *theology is intensely practical*, for the doctrinal section of an Epistle is always followed by practical

exhortations based upon it. According to Paul a true theology *must* lead to right living, and right living in the best sense of the words *must* be based on a true theology.

E.—THE LIFE OF PAUL AND THE ORDER OF THE EPISTLES

We shall endeavour in this section to sketch the life of Paul, showing the order in which the Epistles came to be written, for they do not appear in chronological order in the New Testament, see pp. 116, 117.

(If no book is mentioned, references in this section are to Acts.)

1. *Paul's early life*

Birth and education.—Paul was a Jew of pure Hebrew blood on both sides, and belonged to the tribe of Benjamin (Phil. iii. 5). He was born and brought up at Tarsus, in Cilicia (xxi. 39), where his parents were presumably engaged in business. His father was a Roman citizen, possibly by purchase, or as a reward for services to the Government, and Paul thus inherited many civil rights and privileges (xxii. 25–28). He was taught the art of making tents, or perhaps the weaving of the rough hair-cloth used for their manufacture, but his family must have been one of considerable position, for he received the Jewish equivalent of a university education—he was sent to Jerusalem to become a pupil of the great Gamaliel (xxii. 3). Tarsus was itself a university town, and it is probable that Paul gained there some knowledge of Greek literature and philosophy.

The hope of the Jews.—As a young man his character was without reproach, and even amongst the Pharisees, who with all their defects were truly zealous for religion, he was conspicuous for his piety and devotion. Clever, rich, well connected, and fired with love for his country and its religion, great things were expected from him. Within, at most, a few years of the Crucifixion he was in a position to "vote" against the Christians (xxvi. 10, R.V.), so that he must have been elected a member of the great Jewish Council, or Sanhedrin, at an exceptionally early age. Marriage was regarded among the Jews as so obviously a duty of the good citizen, that it is extremely improbable that he could have secured this position if he had been unmarried. 1 Cor. vii. 8, which suggests that he was unmarried, probably means that he had been a widower for many years; or it may quite well have been that, like the rest of his friends, his wife abandoned him when he became a Christian.

The persecutor.—Paul's life during the first days of Christianity was so closely associated with Jerusalem that it is quite possible that he was there during the Passion Week, and was a witness of the Crucifixion. He was the bitterest of the early opponents of Christianity, and not only took part in the martyrdom of Stephen, but harried the Christians even in distant parts. It is a touching suggestion of Dr. Alexander Whyte's that the reason why in after days he was so deeply interested in the fund for the poor saints of Jerusalem was that it was his persecution which had brought many of them to widowhood or orphanhood and want.

2. *Paul's conversion and qualifications*

Conversion.—The sudden conversion and complete transformation of this persecutor is a testimony to the truth and the power of Christianity that nothing can weaken. The story is familiar, but two or three points should be noted:

(*a*) The crisis was not quite unprepared for, since it is evident from Acts xxvi. 14 that he had been resisting his conscience for some time. The bearing of Stephen in his hour of martyrdom probably started uneasy questionings as to whether Christianity might not after all be true.

(*b*) Though his companions heard the voice, they saw *no man* (ix. 7). Yet for Paul the vision was so distinct that he claimed ever afterwards that *he had seen the Risen Lord* as truly as any of those to whom He appeared between the Resurrection and Ascension (1 Cor. xv. 8). The message of Jesus to him was, according to Paul, as distinct a call to apostleship as that of any of the Twelve; again and again he tells us that he was *called* to be an Apostle (e.g., Rom. i. 1). Hence he contended that he had the full qualifications for apostleship (1 Cor. ix. 1).

(*c*) Acts xxiii. 3–5 and such passages as Gal. iv. 15 suggest that Paul suffered from some defect of eyesight. If so, this was probably an after-effect of that dazzling vision.

Qualifications for work.—Both to Paul and to Ananias the whole incident brought the message that he was to be an apostle to the Gentiles (Acts ix. 15). Paul believed that God had been preparing him for this work from his very birth (Gal. i. 15);

and in several ways he was *peculiarly fitted for missionary work:*

(*a*) Quite apart from any arguments he might be able to urge, *Paul's conversion was a most striking witness* to the truth of Christianity. He had so much to lose by becoming a Christian, and his previous bitterness had been so notorious, that everyone would feel that the evidence that could convince him and the power that could transform him must be overwhelming.

(*b*) His *profound knowledge* of the Old Testament and of the Jewish system qualified him to take the leading part in the great transformation by which the religion of a little nation expanded into a religion for all mankind.

(*c*) His *birth at Tarsus* enabled him to speak Greek with perfect ease, and his *Gentile surroundings* in a busy town gave him larger ideas of the world and wider sympathies than were found in the typical Jew.

(*d*) His *Roman citizenship* gave him a certain social position, and conferred many special rights and privileges wherever he might travel in the Empire.

Sojourn in Arabia.—We are told that after the three days of darkness he testified to Jesus in Damascus (Acts ix. 19, 20). But in verse 22 it is said that he no longer merely testified, but *proved* that Jesus was the Christ. Between verses 21 and 22 we must insert the *sojourn in Arabia* mentioned in Gal. i. 16–18, though Luke omits it, presumably because it belonged to Paul's private life. The "three years" spoken of in Gal. i. 18 need not mean more than one complete year and a part of the years before and after.

It is, of course, possible that this interval was spent in missionary work in those parts, but the convulsion in Paul's life was so complete that we can quite understand that he would need a long period of quiet and of meditation to "find himself" again. Hence it is fairly generally believed that it was now that he wrestled with the great problems of Christian doctrine, and found the answers to great questions that the infant Church had not faced as yet, though they would have to be faced before long, questions such as these: How does Jesus fulfil the Old Testament prophecies concerning the Messiah? How can this Man of Nazareth be the Eternal Son of God? and, How can His Death atone for sin? More than anything at this stage the Church needed a *thinker*, a man with a mind great enough to be capable of understanding the full meaning of Christian truth and the necessity for the Incarnation and Death of Christ. Such a man God provided in Paul, the *great theologian* of Christianity.

3. *Paul the Missionary*

Tarsus and Antioch.—Acts ix. 22–30 shows us that on his return to Damascus plots soon drove him from the city (cf. 2 Cor. xi. 32, 33), and he paid his *first visit to Jerusalem* since his conversion, being introduced to the Church there by Barnabas. Gal. i. 18, 19 tells us that of the leaders he saw only Peter and James, the Lord's brother. After only fifteen days Jewish plots compelled him to retire to Tarsus. As far as can be gathered, he remained in this neighbourhood some seven years, doing missionary work throughout the province. At the end of this time Barnabas took him to Antioch in Syria, where they laboured together for a year with great success (Acts xi. 25, 26).

The fund for the poor Christians of Jerusalem was initiated now, and Paul's *second visit to Jerusalem* was to carry the contribution of the Church at Antioch (Acts xi. 29, 30). It is rather perplexing that Paul should not mention this visit in Galatians; yet it is generally supposed, though Ramsay denies it, that Gal. ii. 1–10 refers to the third visit to Jerusalem, mentioned in Acts xv. 1, 2. This point is discussed on pp. 149, 150.

Paul and Barnabas brought back from Jerusalem John Mark (Acts xii. 25).

First Journey.—Under the guidance of the Spirit, the Church of Antioch now sent out Paul and Barnabas on the *First Missionary Journey* (Acts xiii. 1–3), Mark accompanying them as their attendant. After passing through Cyprus, they landed at Perga, where John, i.e., Mark, deserted them (xiii. 13). They then travelled into the highlands of Asia Minor. At Lystra, Paul was stoned, and it was probably this cruel experience which left his body branded with "the marks of Jesus" (Gal. vi. 17). From Derbe they returned over the same route to Antioch, only omitting Cyprus (Acts xiv. 26).

The chief outcome of this journey was the founding of the Churches at Iconium, Lystra, and Derbe, which with others in those parts were possibly the Churches to which the Epistle to the Galatians was written. In the course of this tour the name *Paul* takes the place of the Apostle's earlier name, *Saul* (xiii. 9).

Circumcision controversy.—Paul and Barnabas stayed at Antioch a considerable time (Acts xiv. 28). Meanwhile the vexed question of Circumcision came to the front, and some think that it was about this date that Paul wrote the Epistle to the *Galatians*, in which case this would be the earliest of his letters (see pp. 145, 146). Acts xv. describes the great Council at Jerusalem, in which Paul took a prominent part, this being, according to the ordinary view, his *third visit to Jerusalem*. The decision of the Council that Gentile converts need not be circumcised was a great victory for the cause that Paul advocated.

Second Journey.—After a further stay in Antioch (Acts xv. 35), Paul and Barnabas decided to revisit the Churches they had founded in Asia Minor. Paul, however, would not consent to take Mark with them, and Barnabas therefore went to Cyprus accompanied by Mark, whilst Paul set out on his *Second Missionary Journey*, with *Silas* for his companion. Striking over the mountains from Antioch, they quickly came to Derbe and Lystra. At Lystra Paul found *Timothy* (Acts xvi. 1), a lad who had apparently been converted on the previous visit, and who now became a life-long companion and fellow-worker. Their natural route was along the great main road that led to Ephesus, and this city was so large and important that Paul was eager to preach there. The Spirit, however, forbade him to preach in that district, which the Romans called the province of Asia, and also prevented him from entering the adjoining province of Bithynia, so that he came eventually to Troas. Here he met *Luke*, for the use of *we* begins at this point (Acts xvi. 10). It was probably what Luke had said to him during the day as to the needs of Macedonia that led to the vision at night of "the man of Macedonia" (Acts xvi. 9, 10). The meaning of the refusal of his wish to preach at Ephesus now became clear—it was more important that a beginning should be made in *Europe*.

Europe.—Crossing over to *Europe*, Paul, Silas, and Timothy founded the Churches at Philippi (where Luke remained behind), Thessalonica, Berœa, Athens, and Corinth (where they stayed some eighteen months). Interesting episodes were the imprisonment at Philippi and conversion of the Philippian jailer, the sermon at Athens, the friendship with Aquila and Priscilla begun at Corinth, and Paul's appearance before Gallio. Whilst they were at Corinth, Paul heard of difficulties in the Church at Thessalonica over the question of the Second Coming of Christ. The two *Epistles to the Thessalonians* were written in quick succession to supplement the rather scanty teaching Paul had been able to give during his brief stay among them.

From Corinth they returned by sea, touching at Ephesus, where they could not stay, and so by way of Cæsarea to Jerusalem. This was the *fourth visit to Jerusalem*, Paul's object this time being to fulfil a vow and keep one of the Jewish feasts (Acts xviii. 18–21). "He went up," i.e., to Jerusalem (*v.* 22), and then returned to Antioch.

Three important points should be noted here:

(*a*) Though Paul contended so strenuously for the freedom of his Gentile converts, he himself still *prized the Jewish religion* in which he had been brought up, visiting the synagogues in every city, and going up to Jerusalem for the festivals when he could.

(*b*) In every place his message was *to the Jews first*, and he only turned to the Gentiles when they had rejected it.

(*c*) Except at Philippi, where it was a question of monetary loss to the owners of the slave girl, the *opposition* was either purely *Jewish* or instigated by Jews. Representatives of the Government, like Gallio, refused to recognize the matter as any concern of theirs, and dismissed the charges brought against Paul by the Jews, on the ground that he was accused of no offence against the law.

Third Journey.—After a brief stay at Antioch (Acts xviii. 23), Paul set out on his *Third Missionary Journey*. Starting, as before, over the mountains, he passed once more through Galatia and Phrygia, and so came to Ephesus. This time he was able to make a long stay there, rather more than two years, in fact. A conspicuous feature of his ministry here was *miracles of healing*, possibly because this city was much given to sorcery and magic.

During his stay at Ephesus Paul received rather disquieting news from Corinth, and a letter also came from the Church there asking for information on a number of points. His reply formed what we know as 1 *Corinthians*. (Some also date *Galatians* from Ephesus, but it is commonly supposed to have been written from Corinth a few months later. Those who believe in the Ephesian origin of the Prison Letters also insert them at this point. See pp. 164–168).

A riot at Ephesus, combined with his uneasiness about the Corinthians, brought his ministry there to a close. He sent Titus in advance, bearing his letter to the Corinthians, and himself soon followed, travelling anxiously through Macedonia. There Titus met him with good news of the Corinthians and the spirit in which they had received his letter. He at once replied in what we call 2 *Corinthians*, and went on more leisurely to Corinth in the wake of this letter. His stay there on this occasion was three months (xx. 3), during which time he probably wrote *Galatians*, though see pp. 108, 146. He was now eagerly looking forward to a brief visit to Jerusalem for Pentecost (xx. 16), after which he would seek to realize the crowning ambition of his life and go to Rome (xix. 21). To prepare the Church there for his visit he wrote the great *Epistle to the Romans*.

Leaving Corinth, he travelled back through Macedonia, picking up Luke once more at Philippi, for *us* and *we* are resumed in chapter xx. 5. Coasting along from Troas, he met the Ephesian elders at Miletus and delivered his solemn address to them, and then pushed on by sea to Cæsarea, impelled all the time by the Spirit, though he knew that trouble awaited him at Jerusalem (xx. 22, 23). He and his party were welcomed at Cæsarea, but his friends implored him not to venture further (xxi. 12).

4. *The arrest of Paul and Cæsarean Imprisonment.*

Arrest.—The journey to the capital was made without mishap, this being his *fifth, and last, visit to Jerusalem.* The leaders of the Church there expressed their personal confidence in him, but warned him that many of the Jewish Christians distrusted him because of his zeal for Gentile freedom. To show that he still approved of Jewish observances for Jewish Christians they urged him to appear in the Temple with four Jewish friends, who at the time had a vow. Unfortunately there were in his party some Gentile converts. These were *not* the men whom he took with him into the Temple, but some of his old enemies raised the cry that he had defiled the Temple by bringing Gentiles into the Court of the Men. A fierce riot ensued, and he was only rescued by the intervention of Claudius Lysias and his troops. The next day he was brought before the Sanhedrin, but the Council was so divided between Pharisees and Sadducees that another disturbance arose. His enemies then arranged to ask that he might be brought before the Sanhedrin again, and a group of forty of them planned to murder him before he reached the council-chamber. See xxi. 17–xxiii. 15.

Imprisonment at Cæsarea.—It chanced, however, that a nephew of Paul's heard of this plot, and disclosed it to Claudius Lysias, though, seeing that he was acquainted with the secrets of the Jews, he himself can hardly have been a Christian. That night Paul was secretly despatched to Cæsarea with a strong escort of troops. Felix, as the Roman Procurator or deputy governor of Palestine, like

Pilate, had his headquarters there. The trial described in Acts xxiv. yielded no result; and as Felix had hopes of a substantial bribe (xxiv. 26), he delayed pronouncing any verdict, so that when he was superseded by Festus at the end of two years, Paul was still a prisoner (xxiv. 27), though he was treated with great consideration (xxiv. 23). This constitutes the *two years' imprisonment at Cæsarea.* It was probably at this time that Luke gathered the materials for his Gospel and the Acts.

Appeal to Cæsar.—The new governor, Festus, soon heard Paul's case, and would have released him, only that he appealed to the Supreme Court of the Empire. King Agrippa and Bernice were also favourably impressed (xxv., xxvi.).

The question arises, *Why did Paul appeal to Cæsar*, a long, risky and costly matter, when liberty was within reach? He seems to have felt that the hostility of the Jews to Christianity was now so great that, until the highest court had pronounced that Christianity was a lawful religion, there would be no cessation of Jewish persecution in Palestine, and wherever else the Jews were numerous enough to make a riot. Further, Paul may have felt that Festus was playing into the hands of his enemies at Jerusalem and meant eventually to surrender him to them (Acts xxv. 9).

Was he rich?—The appeal must have been *exceedingly costly*, just as an appeal to the House of Lords means enormous expenditure here. Paul would have to pay the expenses of himself, his party, and his guards on the voyage to Rome. Arrived there, he had to maintain himself and his companions whilst he waited for his case to come on, and the legal fees would also be very heavy. Only a well-to-do man could undertake such an appeal. Further, the facts that Felix expected a bribe, and that throughout the voyage Paul was treated with great deference, indicate that he was not poor. Yet on his missionary travels he had to work at his trade to maintain himself (xx. 34). It is very likely that his family was rich, and that when he became a Christian his allowances were cut off. But some part of the family property would necessarily fall to him on his father's death, and if his father died about this time, Paul would probably find himself with considerable means. It appears that he chose to spend the money on this appeal, for the fact that the Philippians sent him a gift of money at Rome indicates that he became somewhat straitened financially as the case proceeded.

5. *Voyage to Rome and First Roman Imprisonment*

First Roman Imprisonment.—After a long and hazardous voyage, in which he suffered shipwreck, Paul at length reached *Rome*, and thus entered upon his *First Roman Imprisonment*. Acts xxviii. 30 tells us that he lived there for two years in his own hired house, but says nothing as to the trial and its issue. It was probably during this period that he wrote the prison letters—*Ephesians*, a somewhat general letter to Ephesus and neighbouring Churches; *Colossians*, to meet an insidious heresy which had taken some hold at Colossæ; *Philippians*, to express his thanks for a gift of money; and *Philemon*, to intercede for Onesimus, a runaway slave of Philemon's, who had made his way to Rome. (Some suppose, however, that these Epistles were written from Cæsarea, or even earlier during a supposed imprisonment at Ephesus in the period covered by Acts xix. 23–41. The question is discussed on pp. 164–168.)

The conclusion of Acts, which does not say that he died at the end of the two years in Rome, leaves us to infer that he was released. This is confirmed by the confident hope he expresses in Phil. i. 26, ii. 24, and by many traditions.

6. *Closing period of Paul's life*

Release.—Clement of Rome (A.D. 100) speaks of Paul as coming to "the limit of the West." For an inhabitant of Rome, this phrase could only mean *Spain*, which we see from Rom. xv. 28 that Paul had long wished to visit. There are some faint traditions of a Spanish journey. The Pastoral Epistles also point to visits to his old Churches in Greece and Asia Minor, and some even of those who reject the Pastorals admit that there must be some basis of fact for this.

It is commonly supposed that this interval of freedom lasted five years, and that the journey to *Spain* came first. Paul then visited Crete, Asia Minor, and Corinth. 1 *Timothy* was written to encourage Timothy, who was in charge of the Church at Ephesus. Later he wintered at Nicopolis and wrote from there to *Titus*, who was at work in Crete.

Arrest and Death.—He was then arrested, and

2 *Timothy* was written during his *Second Roman Imprisonment*, when the first trial was over and the end was impending. The spot where he is said to have been beheaded, a little way outside Rome, is now marked by a handsome arch.

7. *The authorship of the Pauline Epistles*

Most of these Epistles are connected together by so many links, and are so closely bound up with the life of Paul, that it is almost impossible to doubt that they were written by him. The only objections that have ever been raised are so trivial and so uninteresting that it is hardly worth while to discuss them. The beginner, at all events, will find it much more profitable to assume that these Epistles are the work of Paul, and devote his time to the study of their teaching.

In the case, however, of the *Pastoral Epistles*, i.e., 1 and 2 Timothy and Titus, the authorship is seriously questioned, and will need to be carefully discussed; and *Ephesians* is also doubted by some. The origin of *Hebrews*, which makes no mention of Paul, also furnishes a very interesting problem.

It will be found best to study the Epistles in the order in which they were written, which is very different from the order of the English New Testament.

Order.—They should probably be arranged as follows:

1st Group.	1 and 2 Thessalonians.
2nd Group.	1 and 2 Corinthians, Galatians, Romans.

3rd Group.	Ephesians, Colossians, and Philemon. Philippians.
4th Group.	1 Timothy, Titus, 2 Timothy.

IMPORTANT DATES IN THE LIFE OF PAUL

The following are the dates assigned by Dr. G. G. Findlay in his *Epistles of Paul the Apostle*, the figures in brackets being those assigned by Dr. C. H. Turner in his great article on the Chronology of the New Testament (Hastings's *Dictionary of the Bible*, Vol. I.):

36. Conversion. (35 or 36.)
38. First visit to Jerusalem after his Conversion and meeting with Peter.
43. Joins Barnabas at Antioch.
46–47. First Missionary Journey. (47).
49. Council at Jerusalem. (49.)
49–52. Second Missionary Journey. (49–52.)
50–51. *1 and 2 Thessalonians.*
52–53. Collision with Peter at Antioch.
53–57. Third Missionary Journey. (52–56).
56–57. *1 and 2 Corinthians, Galatians, Romans.*
57–59. Arrest at Jerusalem and Cæsarean Imprisonment. (56–59.)
59–62. Voyage to Rome and First Roman Imprisonment. (59–62.)
About 62. *Ephesians, Colossians, Philemon, Philippians.*
62. Release.

62–66. Missionary tour, including Spain.
66 (?). 1 *Timothy*, *Titus*, 2 *Timothy*.
66–67. Arrest and Second Roman Imprisonment.
67. Death. (64 or 65.)

Many date the death of Paul in A.D. 64, and several of the closing events of his life correspondingly earlier. Ramsay dates Galatians shortly before the beginning of the Third Journey in A.D. 53. Lake actually dates it before the Council at Jerusalem in A.D. 49. Duncan dates the Prison Epistles, or at least Philippians, from Ephesus, about A.D. 55.

CHAPTER X

The Epistles to the Thessalonians

A.—PAUL'S CONNEXION WITH THE CHURCH AT THESSALONICA

Founding of the Church.—The story of the founding of this Church is told in Acts xvii. 1–10. Immediately after their release from prison at Philippi, Paul and Silas, accompanied by Timothy, moved on to Thessalonica. This is still a large town, notable for its trade in dried figs. The modern name is Saloniki.

The Jewish population was considerable, and Paul, as usual, appealed first to them, preaching in the synagogue on three successive Sabbaths. He won a few converts among the Jews, but more among the Gentile proselytes, including several ladies of position in the town. Moved by jealousy because salvation was being offered to the Gentiles on the same terms as to themselves, the unbelieving Jews secured the help of the roughs and loafers of the place, and attacked the house of Jason, where Paul was lodging. Jason and some others, but not Paul, were brought before the magistrates, or "politarchs," but were discharged when they deposited a sum of money as security for their good behaviour. The situation was so alarming, however, that the little band of Christians hurried Paul and his companions away to Berœa by night.

As he could not go through Macedonia without passing through Thessalonica, Paul must have visited this Church both coming and going on his Third Journey (Acts xx. 1 and 3). Probably he visited it again in the course of the last journey of all which brought him to Nicopolis (Titus iii. 12).

B.—THE FIRST EPISTLE TO THE THESSALONIANS

When written.—After a short stay at Berœa persecution again compelled Paul to escape to Athens, leaving Silas and Timothy at Berœa, apparently because the Jews were less hostile to them than to him (Acts xvii. 13–15). Meanwhile, the persecution of the Christians in Thessalonica continued, and Paul was exceedingly anxious concerning the little Church there left quite unshepherded after only three weeks of his teaching. "Once and again" he was prevented from going back to Thessalonica (1 Thess. ii. 18), and finally he had to send Timothy (1 Thess. iii. 1–5). It is not clear whether Timothy had joined him at Athens and was then sent back to Thessalonica, or whether Paul sent him instructions at Berœa to go back to Thessalonica before coming on to join him. When Silas and Timothy met him once more, it was at Corinth, where Paul had now gone from Athens (Acts xviii. 1, 5). Here he stayed eighteen months, and this letter was written very soon after the arrival of his two friends, for his sufferings at Philippi and at Thessalonica, his loneliness at Athens, and his eager reception of the news

Timothy brought, are all very fresh in his mind (ii. 2, iii. 1–8).

Hence this Epistle was written from *Corinth* shortly after Paul's arrival there on his Second Missionary Journey.

Why written.—Timothy's report was a cheerful one so far as the loyalty of the Thessalonian Church was concerned, but there were three points in it which troubled Paul, and compelled him to write this letter:

1. The Thessalonian Christians were still being bitterly *persecuted* (i. 6, iii. 2–4).

2. Jewish enemies were circulating *malicious reports* to the effect that Paul was a wily and covetous impostor (ii. 1–12).

3. The Thessalonians were greatly perplexed concerning the *Second Coming of Jesus.* They were apparently expecting it at any moment, and, as some of their number had died, they feared that they had lost their share in Christ's triumph (iv. 13–v. 11).

OUTLINE OF I THESSALONIANS

1. *Salutation* from Paul, Silas and Timothy (i. 1).
2. *Thanksgiving* for:
   (*a*) Their Christian character and experience (i. 2–5).
   (*b*) Their faithfulness under persecution (i. 6).
   (*c*) The influence of their heroic endurance in winning others (i. 7–10).
3. *Paul's defence of himself against Jewish slanders* (ii., iii.).

(*a*) His readers knew how unselfishly he laboured in Thessalonica (ii. 1–12).
(*b*) They knew from experience how prejudiced the Jews were (ii. 13–16).
(*c*) He had not forgotten them, but had been prevented from coming, and at last had had to send Timothy (ii. 17–iii. 5).
(*d*) He was so far from forgetting them that Timothy's good report had rejoiced his heart (iii. 6–10).
(*e*) He prays lovingly for them (iii. 11–13).

4. *Teaching on Christian morality* (iv. 1–12).
(*a*) They must shun impurity (iv. 1–8).
(*b*) They must love one another (iv. 9, 10).
(*c*) They must do their daily work faithfully (iv. 11, 12).

5. *Teaching on the Second Coming of Christ* (iv. 13–v. 11).
(*a*) The dead in Christ will share in its glory (iv. 13–18).
(*b*) The children of light must watch and pray (v. 1–11).

6. *Concluding exhortations* (v. 12–25).
7. *Farewell and Benediction* (v. 26–28).

C.—THE SECOND EPISTLE TO THE THESSALONIANS

Its origin.—This letter shows that it was written under very much the same conditions as the first: there was still *persecution* (i. 4–7), and the *Second Coming* was still causing great perplexity (ii. 1–12). It is clear, therefore, that it was written from Corinth very shortly after the first Epistle.

Paul's main reason for writing was that some

members of the Church were so possessed with the idea that Christ was coming immediately that they did not think it worth while to go on with their business, but had thrown up their work, and were living lives of idleness, "sponging" upon their fellows. As a result reproach had fallen upon the Christian cause, and Paul has to rebuke them very sharply.

OUTLINE OF 2 THESSALONIANS

1. *Salutation* from Paul, Silas, and Timothy (i. 1, 2).
2. *References to their persecutions* (i. 3–12).
   (*a*) Thanksgiving for their steadfastness (i. 3, 4).
   (*b*) God will reward them and punish their persecutors (i. 5–10).
   (*c*) Prayer that they may be kept faithful (i. 11, 12).
3. *Teaching on the Second Coming* (ii. 1–12).
   It is not to be yet: there must first be the great *falling away* and the revelation of the Lawless One or *Man of Sin.*
4. *Paul's hopes concerning them* (ii. 13–iii. 5).
   (*a*) God has given them a great calling (ii. 13–15).
   (*b*) He can keep and establish them (ii. 16–iii. 5).
5. *Warnings to the idle and unruly* (iii. 6–15).
   (*a*) He himself had set them an example of honest toil (iii. 6–10).
   (*b*) The idle must, if necessary, be put out of the Church (iii. 11–15).
6. *Farewell benedictions* (iii. 16–18).

D.—THE SPECIAL TEACHING OF 1 AND 2 THESSALONIANS

The Second Coming.—The outstanding feature of these Epistles is obviously their teaching on *the Second Coming of Christ*. We may note:

Its prominence in the thought of the Early Church. It evidently bulked far more largely in the minds of the earliest Christians than it does in the minds of most of us to-day. Paul never committed himself to any definite date, and warned the Thessalonians that it could not be immediately (2 Thess. ii. 2, 3). Yet it is clear that at that time he expected that he and many of his readers would live to see it, for in 1 Thess. iv. 15 he says: "*We* that are *alive*, that *are left* unto the coming of the Lord," and in 1 Cor. xv. 51 he says: "*We* shall not *all* sleep (i.e., die)." But in the interval between the writing of 1 and 2 Corinthians he passed through a serious illness, and 2 Cor. i. 9 makes it clear that he realized then that perhaps he would not live to see the Return, and that he might be one of those who needed to be raised from the dead. Yet the conviction of a splendid and visible triumph of Christ, whether he himself lived to see it or not, was one of his great inspirations to the end.

Passages such as "The Lord is at hand" (Phil. iv. 5) are often quoted as showing that in this matter the whole of the Early Church was seriously mistaken. But we must be careful not to exaggerate. They certainly supposed that the Return was not *very* far distant. Yet our Lord had said, "Lo, I am with you alway" (Matt. xxviii. 20), and some of these passages may refer, not to the final Coming, but to this perpetual coming and abiding presence of Christ.

Order of events.—Paul teaches in 2 Thess. ii. 1–12 that *two great events will precede the Return of Jesus:* (1) *a great apostasy*, when many will fall away from the Faith; (2) *the revelation of the Man of Sin, or Man of Lawlessness.* It is exceedingly difficult to form any definite idea of the way in which these prophecies will be fulfilled. Apparently Paul started from the thought that for the present evil is being held in check. The restraining influence at that time was the system of law and order established under the Roman Government; just as with us the forces of civilization and public opinion, as well as the laws of the nation, keep men's evil passions within certain bounds. But Paul teaches that before the End there will be a great falling away from the Faith, and that, as a result, these restraining influences will break down, so that there will be a great outburst of uncontrolled wickedness and lawlessness.

CHAPTER XI

The Epistles to the Corinthians

A.—CORINTH AS A CENTRE FOR MISSIONARY WORK

Corinth was, and still is, much the largest town in Greece. It is situated on the narrow isthmus which joins the mainland to the large fan-shaped peninsula in the south. In Paul's day it was important—(1) as a *fortress* commanding the narrow neck of land, by which alone an army could march from the north to the south of Greece; (2) as a *port*, with a harbour on each of two seas; (3) as a great *junction* of roads and sea-routes, through which all traffic from Rome to the East must pass; (4) as the *capital* of the Roman province of Achaia; (5) as a special centre of the *worship* of Aphrodite (pronounced Aph-rod-it-e).

A canal for ships has now been cut through the isthmus, but at that time small vessels used to be taken across on rollers. The port is still busy, though not so busy as it was then. With an incessant stream of travellers passing through, the city offered great attractions to the Christian missionary, for if Christianity could be established there, it would be carried in all directions and to many distant lands. At the same time Corinth presented unusual difficulties to the Christian worker, for gross immorality formed part and parcel of the worship of Aphrodite, and the sensuality and vice of Corinth were notorious. Yet the words "Such were some of you," in 1 Cor. vi. 11, following on a long catalogue of dark vices, show that Christianity succeeded in winning its trophies even among the most degraded.

B.—THE FOUNDING OF THE CORINTHIAN CHURCH

Paul's arrival.—The Church was founded by Paul on his Second Missionary Journey (Acts xviii. 1–18). He arrived there alone, somewhat disheartened by his comparative failure at Athens. Either at the synagogue or in seeking work as a maker of tents or tent-cloth he made the acquaintance of a Jew named Aquila and his wife Priscilla, who were of the same occupation as himself, and he gladly made his home with them. They had been expelled from Rome on account of disturbances which had arisen there in connexion with Christianity. It is impossible to say whether they were Christians at this time or not, but they afterwards became prominent workers, and Priscilla has even been suggested as the writer of the Epistle to the Hebrews.

At the end of a few weeks Silas and Timothy arrived from Macedonia, Timothy bringing news of the Thessalonian Church (1 Thess. iii. 5). Paul's spirit revived, and his preaching now became more urgent, partly perhaps because his heart had been stirred by Timothy's report of the persecutions the Thessalonians were suffering at the hands of the Jews.

Jewish opposition.—Things soon came to a head

between Paul and the Jews: he left the synagogue, and began to preach in the house of Justus next door. Many conversions resulted from his work, notably that of Crispus, one of the most prominent Jews in the town.

Either because he was still hankering to return to his friends at Philippi and Thessalonica and the work in Macedonia, or because he was alarmed by the opposition of the Jews, a vision from God came to bid him remain at Corinth, promising him much fruit. His stay finally lengthened out to eighteen months.

Gallio.—The one serious attempt at opposition came to nothing. The Jews brought him before Gallio. the Roman proconsul. He refused to recognize the charge they brought as any concern of his, and took no notice of the horse-play of the Gentile mob when they set upon Sosthenes, the leader of the Jews in this accusation, and beat him. (This is the meaning of the words "Gallio cared for none of these things.") This trial was, however, a matter of far-reaching importance for Paul: Gallio's verdict amounted to *an official declaration that the Roman Government would not allow Christian preaching to be interfered with in that province*. It is quite possible that the very Sosthenes who led the opposition to Paul on that occasion was afterwards converted, for in 1 Cor. i. 1 a Christian named Sosthenes sends greetings to the Corinthian Church.

At the end of eighteen months Paul left Corinth for Jerusalem, sailing straight across to Ephesus and then coasting round to Palestine, probably in one of the ships that were chartered to carry the large numbers of Jews who went to Jerusalem year by year for the Passover (Acts xviii. 18–22).

C.—FIRST EPISTLE TO THE CORINTHIANS

1. *Circumstances which led to the writing of 1 Corinthians*

Apollos.—Aquila and Priscilla were now at Ephesus. Here they met Apollos, an eloquent Jew, who knew something of Christianity. After giving him fuller teaching they encouraged him to go to Corinth, where he was for some time the most conspicuous figure in the Church (Acts xviii. 24–28).

Meanwhile, Paul had set out on his Third Journey (xviii. 23), and had arrived at Ephesus, where he settled for two years (xix).; so that we have to think of the Corinthian Church as being under the charge of Apollos, whilst Paul was busy at Ephesus.

Paul's communication with Corinth.—The two great ports were within easy reach of one another, and travellers were so often passing between them that Paul must have been in fairly close touch with Corinth. But some complicated questions arise, as to the letters and visits that passed between him and the Church there. It is certain, however, that before what we call 1 Corinthians was written, Paul sent them at least one other *letter* which has been lost, for he says in 1 Cor. v. 9, "I wrote to you in my letter," etc. This apparently referred to a case of immorality, and many suppose that a fragment of it has been preserved in 2 Cor. vi. 14–vii. 1, for that passage seems quite out of place there, and refers to the subject of immorality.

Paul seems also to have paid a *flying visit* to Corinth, for as far as Acts tells us the visit paid after the writing of 2 Corinthians would only be the second, yet he says in 2 Cor. xiii. 1, "This is the *third* time I am coming to you." It would, of course, be very easy for him to slip across by sea during his stay at Ephesus.

The crisis.—Before the close of his ministry at Ephesus, things reached a crisis at Corinth. A deputation arrived bringing a *reply* to his lost letter, for he refers to their letter in 1 Cor. vii. 1, and the names of their representatives are mentioned in 1 Cor. xvi. 17. Their reply only partially satisfied him, and it included a number of *questions*.

Just at this time other visitors from Corinth arrived, members of the household of Chloë, and their report was as bad as it could well be (see 1 Cor. i. 11). They told him that the Church was split into factions, that some were busy disparaging him, and that no decided action had yet been taken about the case of immorality.

Paul was intensely distressed and alarmed. Forthwith he wrote what we call 1 *Corinthians*. We gather from 2 Cor. xii. 18 that he despatched it by Titus and another "brother," and left Ephesus for Troas, where he waited in great distress for the return of Titus (see 2 Cor. ii. 12, 13). As he did not come, he pushed on into Macedonia (Acts xx. 1), and met him there.

1 Corinthians was thus written just before Paul's departure from Ephesus on his Third Journey (cf. 1 Cor. xvi. 8).

2. *Chief topics of* 1 *Corinthians*

Divisions.—In chapters i.–iv. Paul deals with *the divisions* in the Church and the *disparaging statements* of his enemies at Corinth. The trouble seems to have arisen in connexion with Apollos, but apparently not through any fault of his, for 1 Cor. xvi. 12 makes it clear that Apollos had come back to Ephesus and was on friendly terms there with Paul, and that he was so far from wishing to foster strife at Corinth that he declined to return just then. Yet it was his ministry, with its philosophical tone and its eloquent diction, that was contrasted with Paul's simple Gospel and unpolished speech. Hence there was a *Paul*-party and an *Apollos*-party. The Judaists had also found their way to Corinth, and as Peter was the leading Apostle engaged in work among Jews, there was a *Peter*-party. Lastly there seems to have been a *Christ*-party, who presumably claimed that they alone were the true followers of Jesus. Possibly, however, the last clause in i. 12 may be a separate sentence in which Paul repudiates the whole controversy, and says concerning himself: "But I am *Christ's*—seeing that Christ is not divided, there should be none of these wretched divisions!"

Paul admits that his preaching was so simple and unpretentious that it perhaps seemed *foolish* (i. 18–25). But *God's wisdom* does not need brilliant speech (i. 26–31). And even in his "simple Gospel" there were deep *mysteries*—the mystery of God's great plan for men's salvation—which only the Spirit could reveal (ii).

But they were not really ready yet for the deep

things: their party-spirit and adoration of particular teachers, as if they could produce spiritual results without God, showed that they were still *childish* (iii. 1–9). Their hope of salvation should be built on Christ, not on any *man* (iii. 10–17). And by making one teacher everything they were *losing* what they might gain from others (iii. 18–23).

Further, both he and Apollos were *God's* servants, and must do the work in the way that would please *God*, whether men admired them or not (iv. 1–13).

Lastly, they were *ungrateful* in discarding him, for, whatever Apollos and others might do for them, he alone was their spiritual "father" (iv. 14–21).

The case of immorality.—In chapters v. and vi. Paul deals with the *case of immorality* and the question of *purity* generally. His lost letter had been written with reference to this, but now he knows that the case was even worse than he had supposed, and he sternly insists on the expulsion of the offender. This case was really a test of Paul's authority in the Corinthian Church. The members were not so lost to religion that they wished to shield a gross sinner, but some of them thought that it was a good opportunity to show that they would not be dictated to by him. Hence chapter v, has been called Paul's *ultimatum* to Corinth, and it achieved its purpose.

This case seems to have given rise to an action in the *law-courts*, for in chapter vi. 1–7 Paul protests against the unseemliness of Christian brethren taking a dispute before a *heathen* court.

Their questions.—Chapters vii. 1–xvi. 4 consist of *Paul's replies to the questions they had asked in their letter.* Several times, but not always, he takes up a new question with the words "Now concerning ——," cf. vii. 1, viii. 1, xii. 1 and xvi. 1.

(*a*) *The question of marriage* (vii.). Is it advisable? Paul distinguishes in his answer between some points on which he feels sure that he is guided by the Spirit, and others on which he can only give his own opinion. On the whole he *advises* against marriage, on the ground that it distracts a man from the service of Christ. He does not hold that there is anything sinful in marriage, or that celibacy is a condition of holiness. His position is this: The world is coming to an end soon—why desire a family that will hardly have time to grow up; or why multiply the anxieties and responsibilities of your life, when there is so little time to accomplish Christ's work?

(*b*) *The question of meat offered to idols* (viii.–x.). The animals sacrificed at the heathen temples were afterwards sold on the butchers' stalls in the market. Was it lawful for a Christian man to eat such meat? Paul replies that an idol is *nothing*, and cannot possibly affect the meat that is offered to it. Yet if a man feels any scruples he ought not to eat this meat. Further, the more strong-minded ought not to offend the scruples of the weak in this matter, but *should be willing to abstain* for their sakes. He instances a parallel in his own life: he was a full Apostle and had a right to claim a maintenance from the Church, yet he worked without pay rather than insist on his rights (ix.). Further, they must remember *how easily the strongest may fall* before temptation (x. 1–13): the "strong," who laugh at the idea of any contamination in idol-meat, may go too far in the risks they take. And, again, if they join in the Lord's Supper, they are *partakers of Christ*—the further they can keep from anything connected with heathenism the better (x. 14–22).

It is obvious that this section helps us directly in considering the question of all indulgences and amusements that are "doubtful," such as the use of alcohol, theatre-going, dancing, etc.

(*c*) *Two questions connected with public worship* (xi.). (1) He lays down the rule that *women* must not appear in a public service with their *heads uncovered.* This is still felt to be a seemly rule, though our reasons are perhaps not the same as Paul's. His reference to "the angels" in verse 10 is very curious, and will be found discussed at great length in the commentaries. It is impossible to say now what he meant by it.

(2) He deals with certain *abuses* that had crept into their observance of *the Lord's Supper.* His account of the Last Supper is very valuable for comparison with those found in the Gospels.

(*d*) *The question of the gifts of the Spirit* (xii.–xiv.). The Corinthians seem to have been rich in striking gifts of the Spirit, such as miracles, healing, preaching, and speaking in strange tongues; and there was rivalry between those possessed of different gifts as to which was the greatest. Paul points out that the Church is one body and needs *all* the gifts, and that it would be foolish if one part of the body were jealous of another (xii.). But the best gift of all is within the reach of all, for it is the loving heart (xiii.). Paul rises to his very highest in this beautiful hymn to Love as the greatest thing in the world. Lastly he says that the gifts most to be desired are not the showy ones, such as speaking in unknown tongues, but those which are most helpful to the Church, such as preaching (xiv.)

(*e*) *The question of the resurrection of the body* (xv.). Some denied that there will be any resurrection of the dead, others wished to know what form it will take. Paul first states the evidence that Jesus rose from the dead and argues that our bodies must rise also, and then goes on to show that the new body cannot be the same body that decayed in the grave, but must be a spiritual body fitted for a spiritual world.

(*f*) *The question of the collection* (xvi. 1–4). He explains his plans for his great fund on behalf of the poor saints in Jerusalem, and urges them to get their contribution ready.

OUTLINE OF I CORINTHIANS

Introduction.

(*a*) *Salutation* from Paul and Sosthenes (i. 1–3).

(*b*) *Thanksgiving and prayer* (i. 4–9).

I.—*Topics suggested by the news brought by the household of Chloë* (i. 10–vi. 20).

(*a*) *The evil of divisions* in the Church, and the injustice of the *disparaging statements concerning his preaching* (i. 10–iv. 21).

(*b*) *The case of immorality* (v., vi.).
(1) The need for prompt action (v.).
(2) Christians should not take their disputes into a heathen court (vi. 1–11).
(3) The absolute duty of purity (vi. 12–20).

II.—*Topics suggested by the questions in their letter* (vii. 1–xvi. 4).

(*a*) *Is marriage advisable* (vii.)?
(*b*) *Ought Christians to eat meat that has been offered to idols* (viii.–x.)?
(*c*) *Matters of public worship* (xi.).
(1) May women appear with their heads uncovered (xi. 1–16)?
(2) Reproof of abuses in their observance of the Lord's Supper (xi. 17–34).
(*d*) *Which are the greatest gifts of the Spirit* (xii.–xiv.)?
(1) The Church needs all (xii.).
(2) The best is Love (xiii.).
(3) Of the others, seek those which will help the Church most (xiv.)
(*e*) *The question of the resurrection of the body* (xv.).
(*f*) *His wishes concerning the collection* for the poor saints of Jerusalem (xvi. 1–4).

Conclusion.

(*a*) *Plans* for himself and Timothy (xvi. 5–11).
(*b*) *References* to various friends (xvi. 12–18).
(*c*) *Greetings* from Ephesus (xvi. 19–21).
(*d*) *Benediction* (xvi. 23).

D.—SECOND EPISTLE TO THE CORINTHIANS

1. *Circumstances which led to the writing of 2 Corinthians*

The interval.—After despatching 1 Corinthians, Paul left Ephesus and waited at Troas some months for the return of Titus with further news from Corinth. 2 Cor. ii. 12, 13 shows us that he found an attractive field of work, but that he was so oppressed with anxiety concerning the Corinthian Church that, as Titus did not appear, he crossed over to Macedonia to meet him the sooner.

During this interval Paul experienced his first grave illness, and all but died. He describes in 2 Cor. i. 8–10 how this experience affected his thought: he realized for the first time that perhaps he would not live to see the Lord's Return, and that he might be among those who would have to be raised from the dead.

Arrival of Titus.—At length, to his immense relief, Titus arrived. His report of the Corinthians was in many ways most cheering: 1 Corinthians had been well received, the majority of the Church had pronounced the sentence he had asked for on the man guilty of immorality, and the letter had produced a great change of feeling towards Paul. He expresses in 2 Cor. viil 6–16 the delight that he felt at the news. Further, the culprit had accepted his punishment so humbly and was now so penitent that Paul could recommend the Church to receive him back into membership (2 Cor. ii. 5–11). [We assume that this was the same culprit as the one referred to in 1 Corinthians.]

Disquieting features.—Yet there were some disquieting features in the report of Titus: (*a*) the collection for Paul's great fund was not completed, and time was being lost; (*b*) there was still an important section bitterly opposed to him; (*c*) more Judaists had arrived, probably from Jerusalem, to strengthen the Peter-party, bringing with them letters of commendation (2 Cor. iii. 1). Paul's enemies were ridiculing and disparaging him in every possible way: his appearance was poor, his speech was unpolished, he was no Apostle, and he had claimed no maintenance from the Church only because he knew that he had no right to it—such were the slanders they circulated.

Obviously there was need enough of a further letter. Our 2 Corinthians was written without delay there in Macedonia, and Titus started again for Corinth, accompanied this time by some Macedonian Christian of whom Paul writes in the most glowing terms in chapter viii. 18–24. Many suppose that this was Luke, whose home at this time was almost certainly at Philippi in Macedonia (see pp. 47, 48).

2. *Is 2 Corinthians a single Epistle?*

There are two passages which seem so out of keeping with the rest of the Epistle that many question whether they really belong to it.

vi. 14–vii. 1.—If we read chapter vi. 11–13 and then pass on to chapter vii. 2, the connexion of thought is perfect. The intervening verses, chapter vi. 14–vii. 1, relate to an entirely different subject, immorality, and quite break the connexion. The subject of these verses suggests that they were probably part of the lost letter of Paul referred to in 1 Cor v. 1 and on p. 129, and that by some accident they slipped into the text here at a very early date. This view is very generally taken.

x.–xiii.—The concluding chapters, x.–xiii., also create a difficulty. They form an exceedingly severe attack upon his enemies, that seems strangely out of place in a letter of reconciliation in which he expresses unbounded delight at the better feeling that now existed at Corinth, and in which he also appeals to them to help this fund. Some believe that these four chapters are another portion of the lost letter, or part of yet another letter, for it is possible that these were four letters in all from Paul to this Church. Those who still regard them as belonging to this Epistle plead that they may have been intended only for the hostile faction, and not for the whole Church at Corinth.

3. *Interesting passages in 2 Corinthians*

Epistles of commendation.—In chapter iii. 1–3 Paul shows the contrast between himself and the newly arrived Judaizers, with their "letters of commendation" to introduce them to the Church. He, at least, needed no such credentials, for the Corinthian Christians themselves were his letter of commendation, for none who knew what he had accomplished in Corinth needed any further evidence that he was a true servant of God.

His unpaid work.—His enemies asserted that the reason why he asked for no salary at Corinth was that he was no Apostle, and knew that he had no right to it. He replies in chapter xi. 7–9. "Was it a sin that I made no charge upon you, and tided over my poverty with the willing gifts that came to me from Macedonia?" In verse 20 he continues: "You seem to think that if a man plunders you it is a proof that he is a genuine Apostle, and you accept him as such without further question!"

His sufferings.—In chapter xi. 21–33 he compares himself very reluctantly with his enemies, and says: "I hate to seem to boast, and all these comparisons are foolish. Yet if I *must* compare my claim to be an Apostle with theirs, I am as pure-blooded a Jew as any of them. And if it is a matter of toil, peril and suffering endured for the cause of Christ, it will be difficult to match my record." This list of his perils and persecutions is very interesting, because it adds a great deal to the information given in Acts. Up to the point now reached in Acts (xx. 1) Luke mentions only the stoning at Lystra, one beating with rods at Philippi, and the escape from Damascus, which Paul adds as an afterthought at the end of the list. This fact confirms what was said on pp. 86–88, that Acts was not meant to be a biography of Paul, but a history of the progress of Christianity.

His visions.—His enemies boasted of their visions. Paul apologizes again for making comparisons, but if he must speak of his visions, he can tell of one more remarkable than any of theirs (xii. 1–5). We have no other mention of this vision, but the experience was so extraordinary that it might have tempted him to pride, and Paul believed that it was in order that he "should not be exalted overmuch" that God permitted him to be tormented all his days by his "thorn in the flesh" (xii. 7–10).

The thorn in the flesh.—There has been endless speculation as to what constituted this "thorn in the flesh.' Amongst the suggestions are: (1) prostrating headaches; (2) attacks of malaria or shivering ague; (3) fits of epilepsy; (4) ophthalmia, an eye complaint that would greatly disfigure him; (5) proneness to sensual desires. Either the second or the third seems to be the most probable. Two or three little touches suggest that he suffered at times from some complaint that was rather repulsive to onlookers and very humiliating to himself.

OUTLINE OF 2 CORINTHIANS

Introduction (i. 1–11).

(*a*) *Greeting* from himself and Timothy (i. 1, 2).

(*b*) *Thanksgiving* and good wishes (i. 3–7).

(*c*) *News* of his grave illness (i. 8–11).

I. *His reply to the charge of fickleness* (i. 12–ii. 17).

(*a*) It was not fickleness which prevented his coming to Corinth when they expected him, but a wish to spare them unpleasantness (i. 12–ii. 4).

(*b*) He has been intensely anxious about them (ii. 12–17).

[The guilty man may now be restored (ii. 5–11).]

II.—*His defence of his ministry at Corinth* (iii. 1–vi. 10).

(*a*) His ministry was faithful to the Scriptures (iii.).

(*b*) It was entrusted to him by God, in spite of his frail body (iv.)

(*c*) He longs for the end, but his message is the sacred one of reconciliation between God and men, hence, at all costs, he must continue to preach it (v. 1–vi. 10).

III.—*His appeal to their hearts* (vi. 11–13, vii. 2–16).

(*a*) He longs for cordial relations with them (vi. 11–13 and vii. 2–4).

(*b*) The good news brought by Titus has greatly delighted him (vii. 5–16).

[vi. 14–vii. 1 does not appear to belong to the Epistle.]

IV.—*His appeal for his fund* (viii. and ix.).

V.—*His defence against his slanderers* (x. 1–xiii. 10).

(*a*) He can act strongly as well as write strongly (x. 1–11).

(*b*) He was no interloper like these newcomers: Corinth was part of his field (x. 12-18).

(*c*) Was the fact that he took no pay a proof that he was not an Apostle? (xi. 1–20).

(*d*) Could any of his enemies show such a record of toil and suffering for Christ's sake (xi. 21–33)?

(*e*) Could any of them point to such striking visions (xii. 1–10)?

(*f*) His life among them showed that he was a true Apostle (xii. 11–13).

(*g*) He is coming shortly and, if necessary, will show no mercy (xii. 14–xiii. 4).

(*h*) They, at any rate, should recognize him as an Apostle, for salvation had come to them through him (xiii. 5–10).

Conclusion and Benediction (xiii. 11–14).

CHAPTER XII

THE EPISTLE TO THE GALATIANS

A.—WHO WERE THE GALATIANS?

The Readers.—The most interesting question connected with this Epistle is to decide who the Galatians were. Ordinary Bible maps show a district marked "Galatia" with Lycaonia to the south of it. But for purposes of government the Romans grouped several districts in one province, which they called "Galatia." Did Paul mean by Galatia the ancient country or the Roman province? If he meant the country, the Galatians belonged to towns like Ancyra in the north—this is the *North Galatian theory*. If he meant the Roman province, the Galatians were the Churches of Antioch in Pisidia, Iconium, Lystra and Derbe, founded on his First Journey—this is the *South Galatian theory*.

Until some forty years ago it was generally taken for granted that the Epistle was written to Northern Galatia, but Sir William Ramsay then argued very powerfully for the South Galatian view, and this is now widely accepted, though still not universally.

For South Galatia.—Ramsay's chief arguments are as follows:

(*a*) Paul used Roman provincial names, e.g.,

"Asia," "Macedonia," "Achaia," so that he probably used the word "Galatia" in the Roman sense.

(*b*) The Churches of Iconium, etc., were so important that Paul would be likely to write to them.

(*c*) If he wished to do so, "Galatians" was the only term that would include all four—Antioch, Iconium, Lystra and Derbe.

(*d*) North Galatia was out of the way, and if Churches existed there, they were so unimportant that Paul would not be likely to devote an important Epistle to them.

(*e*) Special light is thrown on some of the expressions in this Epistle if we suppose that Paul was writing to South Galatia, e.g., "the marks of Jesus" (vi. 17) would be the result of the stoning at Lystra, which they would remember.

Against South Galatia.—The objections urged by such writers as the late Dr. G. G. Findlay are that:

(*a*) In Acts xvi. 1–5 Luke has described a visit to Derbe and Lystra, and verse 6 seems to mean that in going "through the region of Phrygia and Galatia" they were breaking fresh ground. But the only fresh ground in Galatia was to the north.

(*b*) Paul did not write to Churches according to their size, e.g., he wrote to the small Church at Colossæ, but not to the strong Church at Tarsus.

(*c*) If the Galatians were the Churches of Iconium, etc., Barnabas had a share in founding them. Yet Paul never refers to the fact, although he mentions Barnabas in this Epistle three times.

(*d*) Calculating by certain references in Galatians and comparing with Acts, Ramsay has to date the Epistle before Paul started on his Third Journey, i.e., in A.D. 52 or 53; but on the other view it cannot have been written until far on in the Third Journey, probably from Corinth in A.D. 56 or 57, shortly after 2 Corinthians and just before Romans, Now one half of Galatians is very like 2 Corinthians and the other half is very like Romans, and to say that it was written three or four years before either of them is almost like asking us to suppose that the second volume of a book was written three or four years before the first and third. This matter of date is a very weighty objection to Ramsay's theory, though it is sometimes met by supposing that Romans i.–xiv. was written earlier than the form of that Epistle which we possess.

The controversy still continues. The majority of scholars certainly accept Ramsay's view that it was South Galatia to which Paul wrote, though some important ones still favour North Galatia. Even those who accept Ramsay's view are not in all cases satisfied with a very early date for the Epistle, and some attempt to combine the southern destination with the familiar date, A.D. 56 of 57.

B.—CIRCUMSTANCES WHICH LED TO THE WRITING OF GALATIANS

Judaists.—Paul's enemies, the Judaists, had been particularly busy in Galatia, and had worked even more mischief there than at Corinth. They had denied his Apostleship, and had circulated the same kind of disparaging statements as at Corinth. But, what was far worse, they had induced many of the Galatian Christians to be circumcised and put themselves completely under the Jewish Law.

Paul was terribly distressed, and this letter is partly a defence of his Apostleship, but chiefly a protest against the circumcision of any Gentile Christian, and an appeal to the Galatian Churches to return to the simple Gospel which he had preached.

C.—THE CONTENTS OF GALATIANS

His Apostleship.—In chapter i. 11–ii. 21 *Paul defends his claim to be an Apostle.* In 2 Cor. x–xiii. he pointed to his labours, sufferings, and successes as the proof of his Apostleship. Here he goes back to the beginning of his ministry, and argues that he was a true Apostle because *he had been called by Christ Himself*, and not appointed by men, as Matthias was (Acts i. 26). He seeks to show that *he owed nothing to the Jerusalem Apostles*, and is thus led to describe the whole of his association with them. He became an Apostle by the direct call of Christ (i. 12), and when he was converted he did not go to Jerusalem, but into Arabia (i. 17), where Christ trained him for the work in solitude. It was three years before he went to Jerusalem at all, and then he stayed only a fortnight, and saw only Peter of the original Apostles (i. 18–24). It was fourteen years from his conversion before he saw any of the Apostles at Jerusalem again. This time he did consult them, but only because he wished to work in harmony with them, not because he needed their permission to preach. They taught him nothing fresh, but quite approved of the work he was doing; in fact, James, Peter and John recognized him as an equal, and agreed that he should take the Gentile field, whilst they worked among the Jews (ii. 1–10).

Further, he was so far from depending on them for authority to preach, that when he met Peter next, this time at Antioch, he rebuked him publicly for yielding to Jewish prejudice and refusing to eat with Gentile Christians (ii. 11–14).

Circumcision.—The second great topic is *the lapse of the Galatians, and their weakness and folly in accepting the Jewish Law and consenting to be circumcised.* This occupies chapters iii. 1–v. 12, but chapter iv. 12–20 is a parenthesis in which he appeals to their old love for him, and warns them that the Judaists are flattering and courting them only to enslave them.

The chief points in the argument are as follows: You were saved by faith *before* you were circumcised (iii. 2), just as Abraham, too, was saved by *believing* God, and not by circumcision (iii. 6–9). Indeed, *no one* has ever been saved by performing these ceremonies (iii. 10–14). God saved Abraham 430 years *before* the Law of Moses came into existence, so that the Law cannot cancel God's promise to those who believe (iii. 15–22). Yet the Law did serve *one* good purpose: it led men to realize their *need of a Saviour* (iii. 23–29).

But God means men to be His *children.* The period from Moses to Christ was like a child's *minority*, when he does not possess his full rights. But now that Christ has come, God means men to enjoy their rights as His children and heirs. It is *foolish* of you, who have known what it is to be God's children, to put yourselves under the Law (iv. 1–11).

Do you wish to call yourselves *children of Abraham*? Remember that he had *two kinds* of children—a *free-born* son by Sarah, and a *slave-child* by Hagar. If you accept the Law, you may be children of Abraham, but only slave-children. But if you imitate his faith, you will be his free-born children (iv. 21–v. 1).

Lastly, if you accept circumcision, you *reduce the Cross to nothing*, for you are not trusting to Christ to save you, but to circumcision (v. 2–12).

It is obvious that this teaching bears directly upon the present-day question of Ritualism.

Christian Morals.—Paul has been declaring that Christ has made them free from the *Jewish* Law. But that does not mean that they are free from the *moral law*, or that sin does not matter: there is still the law of *love* (v. 13–15); and if their life comes from the Spirit of God, it must produce the *fruits of the Spirit*, and not the works of the flesh (v. 16–25).

D.—INTERESTING POINTS IN GALATIANS

Galatians and Acts.—The comparison of Gal. i. and ii. with Acts shows some striking differences. Luke does not mention the visit to Arabia, presumably because it belonged to Paul's private life, but it should come in between verses 22 and 23 of Acts ix.

Gal. i 18–24 refers to the same visit to Jerusalem as Acts ix. 26–30. The two accounts differ considerably, but can be reconciled.

It is a great question whether Gal. ii. 1–10 corresponds to Acts xv. 1, 2, or Acts xi. 29, 30. Seeing that the subject discussed was the position of the Gentile Christians, it is natural to suppose that it refers to the Council of Jerusalem (Acts xv. 1, 2)—indeed, this was hardly questioned before Ramsay's South Galatian controversy began. The question then arises, Why does Paul ignore the visit described in Acts xi. 29, 30, especially as he professes to be describing *everything* that passed between him and the Jerusalem Apostles? The reply may be that he only came to bring a contribution from Antioch; the visit was very hasty; the Church was just passing through the persecution in which James the brother of John was martyred and Peter was imprisoned (Acts xii. 1–3); probably every Apostle had fled from Jerusalem; and it is quite possible that Paul and Barnabas handed over their gift without entering the city at all.

Or another explanation that now finds considerable support is that there was *no* visit to Jerusalem in Acts xi. 29, 30. Those verses may merely describe the foretelling of a famine and preparations to assist when the need should actually arise, which was not till Acts xv. 1.

Paul's infirmity.—In Gal. iv. 13 Paul says that on his first visit to the Galatians he came to them through some sickness, which apparently made his appearance rather forbidding. Ramsay conjectures that he had caught *malaria* at Perga, and went to Iconium, etc., among the mountains to shake it off. Yet if the Galatian Churches were those of Iconium, etc., they all saw him after the *stoning* at Lystra, and that would make his appearance repulsive enough for some time afterwards. Some have thought that the reference to plucking out their eyes (Gal. iv. 15) indicates that it was some *eye trouble* which disfigured him. But this is only a strong figure of speech, meaning that they were ready to do anything for him, and should not be pressed in the literal sense.

Large letters.—In Gal. vi. 11 the R.V. reads: "See with *how large letters* I have written unto you." Paul is writing the closing verses with his own hand, and draws attention to the difference between the neat writing of the scribe and his own, which was rather large. Some have thought that this too was a result of defective eyesight, but many whose sight is perfect write a large hand. It should not be forgotten that he was engaged in hard manual toil, which is not usually favourable to elegant penmanship.

OUTLINE OF GALATIANS

Introduction (i. 1–10).

(*a*) *Salutation*, but *no thanksgiving* (i. 1–5).

(*b*) His *sorrow* at their lapse and *warning* against false teaching (i. 6–10).

I.—*His defence of his Apostleship* (i. 11–ii. 21).

(*a*) *It was conferred, not by the Church, but by the direct call of Christ* (i. 11–17).

(*b*) *He owed nothing to the Jerusalem Apostles* (i. 18–ii. 21).

(1) His first visit was very brief (i. 18–24).

(2) On the second visit they recognized him as an equal (ii. 1–10).

(3) He rebuked Peter for a fault when they met at Antioch (ii. 11–21).

II.—*His protest against the circumcision of the Galatians* (iii. 1–v. 12).

(*a*) *To be circumcised now contradicts their previous experience* (iii. 1–5).

(*b*) *Circumcision is unnecessary* (iii. 6–29).

(1) Abraham was not save by circumcision, but by *faith* (iii. 6–9).

(2) The Law *saves* no one, for none can obey it perfectly (iii. 10–14).

(3) It cannot cancel *God's promise* to believing Abraham (iii. 15–18).

(4) It only serves to make men feel their *need of a Saviour* (iii. 19–29).

(*c*) *Circumcision is a backward step* (iv. 1–11 and iv. 21–v. 1).

(1) Now that Christ has come God wishes men to enter into their rights as His *free children* (iv. 1–11).

(2) If they wish to be children of Abraham, they should be like his *free-born* son, not like his *slave*-child (iv. 21–v. 1).

(*d*) *Circumcision is disloyalty to Christ* (v. 2–12), for if circumcision is to save them, the Cross becomes nothing.

[Parenthesis: Appeal to their former love for him, and warning that the Judaists are only trying to entrap them (iv. 12–20).]

III.—*Practical exhortations* (v. 13–vi. 10).

(*a*) They are *free* in Christ, yet the *law of love* remains (v. 13–15).

(*b*) Their new life is *derived from the Spirit;* it must show *the fruits of the Spirit* (v. 16–26).

(*c*) Miscellaneous *counsels* (vi. 1–10).

Conclusion (vi. 11–18).

(*a*) *Summary* of the leading ideas (vi. 11–17).

(*b*) *Benediction* (vi. 18).

CHAPTER XIII

The Epistle to the Romans

A.—CHRISTIANITY IN ROME

Rome in Church History.—In spite of the Protestant Reformation, Rome is still the head of the largest division of Christendom, the Roman Catholic Church. It did not easily gain this position, for in the early centuries there was a long struggle between the five great Christian centres—Jerusalem, Antioch, Alexandria, Rome, and Byzantium (now known as Constantinople). Constantinople held out longest, and was sometimes supreme; yet as a centre of Christianity it is now merely the nominal and disputed head of the stagnant Greek Church, with a "Patriarch" (or Archbishop) who, until the revolution in Turkey, had for centuries been appointed by the *Mohammedan* Sultan of Turkey, whilst the Pope of Rome is still the greatest human power in the Christian world.

Paul's interest.—In Paul's day there was not even a Bishop of Rome, still less a Pope. But although Christianity was already established there, the city fascinated him, and for years he longed to visit it. He thought of it with its vast population and its enormous influence as the capital of an empire that embraced the whole civilized world, besides great nations that were still barbarian, and he saw that the future of Christianity depended very largely on the hold that it secured there.

B.—THE ORIGIN OF THE CHURCH AT ROME

Traditions.—We have no reliable story of the founding of the Church at Rome. The Roman Catholic tradition is that Peter fled to Rome after his imprisonment by Herod (Acts xii. 17), and remained there for twenty-five years as its first Bishop. This legend seems to have been fabricated to buttress up the claim of the Pope to supremacy. If Peter went to Rome so early, is it conceivable that Luke for whom the arrival of the Gospel there was the great climax, would not have mentioned it in Acts? And if Peter was at the head of the Church in Rome when Paul wrote, is it conceivable that he would not have mentioned him in this Epistle?

Pentecost.—The New Testament throws a little light on the history of the Church. From Acts ii. 10 it appears that there were "sojourners from Rome, both Jews and proselytes" among those present on the day of Pentecost. Presumably some of these were among Peter's converts, and they would carry the Gospel back with them. (In this limited sense Peter *was* the founder of the Roman Church.) The Church would also grow by frequent arrivals of Christians from the provinces, for there was a constant drift towards Rome, just as there is towards London. Yet converts must also have been won from the heathen population, for writing from Rome in Phil. iv. 22, Paul sends greetings from some of "Cæsar's household," showing, on the ordinary interpretation of these words, that Christianity had gained adherents in the retinue of the Emperor himself.

Jewish or Gentile?—It is a little difficult to determine whether this Church consisted mainly of Jewish or of Gentile Christians. The Jewish population in Rome was large, and there are several indications in the Epistle that the Jewish section of the Church was very influential, if it was not more numerous than the Gentile.

(1) Paul does not write as if the majority of his readers had once been heathen, as he does, for instance, in 1 Thessalonians.

(2) He deals very fully with the special difficulties which the Christian Faith would present to Jews.

(3) He quotes freely from the Old Testament.

It seems clear that the Roman Christians were familiar with the Old Testament and had a good deal of sympathy with Jewish ideas. Yet the Church can hardly have been predominantly Jewish:

(1) Numerous as they were, Jews were only a small part of the total population of Rome.

(2) Paul states that his interest in them was due to the fact that they formed part of his field as the Apostle to the Gentiles (i. 13, xv. 15, 16).

(3) He virtually calls them Gentiles in chapters i. 5, 6 and xi. 13.

The probability is, therefore, that the great majority were Gentiles, but that a considerable proportion of them had been *proselytes*, or converts to Judaism, before they became Christians.

C.—CIRCUMSTANCES WHICH LED TO THE WRITING OF ROMANS

When written.—Paul states in Rom. i. 10 and xv. 28, that he was hoping to visit Rome very shortly, and this Epistle was meant to introduce him to the Church there.

Now Acts xix. 21 tells us that when he was leaving Ephesus after his long stay he purposed to go to Rome, but left that he must first run across to Macedonia and Achaia, and expecially to Corinth, and that he must also go to Jerusalem for Pentecost. When he reached Corinth he stayed there three months (Acts xx. 3). As there seemed then to be only the visit to Jerusalem between him and his visit to Rome, that would be the natural time to write this Epistle. We therefore conclude that it was written from Corinth immediately after he had written Galatians. This is confirmed by the close resemblance in the teaching of the two Epistles, for Romans seems to be the finished treatise of which Galatians was the rough draft, except that there is none of the deep feeling that had been roused in him by the lapse of the Galatian Christians.

D.—THE TEACHING OF ROMANS

Letter or treatise?—Romans is more like a treatise than any other Epistle of Paul, although it opens as a letter (i. 1–17), and closes with personal references and greetings (xv. 14–xvi. 23). It consists almost entirely of a long and careful discussion of the great doctrines of Salvation: the theme is the Gospel as "the power of God unto salvation to every one that believeth, to the Jew first and also the Greek" (i. 16).

1. *The Doctrine of the Epistle* (i. 18–xi. 36)

Universal guilt.—Paul sets out to prove that *all men need salvation*, since none have succeeded in reaching righteousness (i. 18–iii. 20). (1) He deals with the *Gentiles*, or *heathen*; they knew something of God, yet they had fallen into idolatry (i. 18–23); and, as a result, their moral nature had become depraved and they had sunk to the most revolting vices (i. 24–32). (2) He shows that the *Jews* also are guilty: God will not overlook their guilt, for many of them were hypocrites, and circumcision had not touched their hearts (ii.). They were privileged to possess the Scriptures, yet the Scriptures themselves condemned them, for the Old Testament passages quoted in chapter iii. 10–18 describing man's guilt were written *by* Israelites *about* Israelites. Thus both Jews and Gentiles are guilty (iii. 19).

God's remedy.—Seeing that men have failed, Paul discusses in chapters iii. 21–v. 21 *God's remedy for sin*. This consists of *justification or pardon given by God to those who believe*. God longed to forgive sinners, but could not do so justly until the guilt of sin had been recognized. In order to make free forgiveness possible, God took the consequences of sin upon Himself in the Person of Christ (iii. 25, 26). Hence salvation is not by men's works or merits, but by *faith* or trust in Christ's Death; and this faith is just as possible for the heathen as for the Jews (iii. 27–31).

The Jews objected that this doctrine reduced the Old Testament system to nothing, and contradicted the Scriptures (iii. 31). But in Chapter iv. Paul shows that it agrees with the Old Testament, for *Abraham* was accepted by God because he *believed* (iv. 3), and further, at that time he was *uncircumcised*, like any Gentile (iv. 10). The promise was made to him because he was a man of *faith*, and the true successors to his promise are those who imitate his *faith*, whether they are Jews or Gentiles (iv. 10–25).

Clearly, if faith brings us this pardon, it ought also to bring *peace*, *hope*, and *joy* (v. 1–3); for if God has loved us so greatly in our sin, we may be sure that He will do still more for us now (v. 6–11).

Does it seem impossible that the *merits* of *Christ* should bring such great blessings to the *whole* race? Remember how the *sin* of one man, *Adam*, brought misery upon the *whole* race (v. 12–21).

The new life.—Paul now describes *the believer's new life in Christ* (vi.–viii.).

(1) It ought to be a *sinless life* (vi.). Those who say that it will not matter if we sin, because God delights to forgive, completely misunderstand the Atonement. To be baptized into Christ's name and believe in His death is to *die to sin*, as He did; so that it is *wrong* for the Christian to sin (vi. 1–11). The Christian receives a *new kind* of life in Christ, and sin shall not have dominion over him; so that it is *unnecessary* for him to sin (vi. 12–14). Lastly, sin *does not pay*, so that it is *foolish* to sin (vi. 15–23).

(2) Though the new life must be a good life, *it need not be a slavish life of obedience to the Jewish*

Law: the Christian is as free from this as a widow is from her dead husband (vii. 1–6). To show how happy a release this is, Paul describes his constant failure and disappointment whilst he was trying to win salvation by keeping the Mosaic Law (vii. 7–25).

(3) The true Christian *cannot help trying* to live the good life, because *the Spirit* is in his heart, moulding his life, reminding him that he is God's child, and helping his infirmity (viii. 1–17).

(4) Lastly, *he will succeed in living the good life*, because his salvation has been *God's purpose* for ages, a purpose that He will not easily abandon, and because nothing can change *God's love* towards him (viii. 18–39).

Unbelieving Israel.—In chapters ix.–xi. Paul faces *the problem of unbelieving Israel.* How can God be just if He casts off His chosen people, and how can Christianity be true if almost all Israel rejects it? Paul replies:

(1) Even if God chose to cast off Israel now *He would not be unjust*, for He is our Maker and may, in theory at least, do what He will with men (ix.).

(2) Their rejection is *their own fault*: they *deserve* to be cast off, because of their obstinacy and unbelief (x.).

(3) Yet God has *not* cast off the nation *as a whole*, for many Jews, such as Paul himself, had become Christians (xi. 1–6).

(4) Further, the unbelief of the Jews had one good result—the Gospel had been taken to the *Gentiles* (xi. 7–12).

(5) But if God could graft *foreign* branches (the Gentiles) into His tree, surely He could graft the

original branches (the Jews) back again. Thus Paul looks forward to a time when *the nation of Israel will return* to God through Christ (xi. 13–36).

2. *The Practical Exhortations* (xii. 1–xv. 13)

The Christian's daily life.—According to Paul, theology should result in right living, and he devotes the remainder of the Epistle to the practical life of the Christian. Note the words "I beseech you *therefore*, brethren," with which he begins this section. The chief topics are:

(*a*) *The consecrated life*, as the natural result of so great a salvation (xii.).

(*b*) *Obedience to the Government*, which, as we saw on p. 125, Paul regarded as God's instrument to restrain sin (xiii. 1–7). [Later on, when the Revelation was written, the worship of the Emperor and the persecution of Christianity by the Government had begun, so that in that book the Roman Government is "the Beast," the great enemy of Christianity.]

(*c*) The duties of *honesty* and *love* (xiii. 8–14).

(*d*) The question of eating *meat offered to idols* and of observing *special days*, such as Jewish festivals. The "strong" must bear with the "weak," so that strong and weak, Jew and Gentile, may dwell together as Christians (xiv. 1–xv. 13).

E.—THE CONCLUSION OF ROMANS

Greetings.—Chapter xvi. contains greetings to many friends, including Aquila and Priscilla. As these two were at Ephesus in Acts xviii. 24–26, some suppose that this Epistle was sent to several Churches with a different conclusion in each case, and that this chapter was meant for Ephesus. It is also said that Paul could not have had so many friends in Rome. But Aquila and Priscilla came from Rome (Acts xviii. 2), and may quite well have returned there by this time. And Paul must have known many of the Roman Christians, by name at any rate, just as every one to-day knows many who live in London. At the same time certain MSS. indicate that slightly modified and abreviated forms of the Epistle found their way to some of the other Churches.

Note the repeated *Benedictions* in chapters xv. 13, 33, xvi. 20, and xvi. 24 (omitted in the R.V.), and the two great *Doxologies* in chapters xi. 33–36 and xvi. 25–27. Note also that Tertius, the scribe to whom Paul dictated the Epistle, mentions his name and sends his greeting (xvi. 22).

OUTLINE OF ROMANS

Introduction (i. 1–17).
- (*a*) *Salutation* (i. 1–7).
- (*b*) *His interest in the Romans* (i. 8–17).

I. *The Christian Doctrine of Salvation* (i. 18–xi. 36).
- (*a*) *The universal need of salvation* (i. 18–iii. 20).
  - (1) The *Gentiles* are guilty (i. 18–32).
  - (2) So are the *Jews* (ii. 1–iii. 20).
- (*b*) *God's plan for man's salvation* (iii. 21–v. 21).
  - (1) The meaning of *Justification by Faith* (iii. 21–31).
  - (2) An illustration from *Abraham*, who was saved by *faith* (iv.) .
  - (3) Such love of God will supply *all* that we need (v. 1–11).

(4) The curse that came on all through *Adam* shows that blessing may come to all through Christ (v. 12–21).

(*c*) *The new life of the Christian* (vi.–viii.).

(1) It must be *free from sin* (vi.).

(2) Yet it is *not slavish obedience* to the Jewish Law (vii.).

(3) The sinless life *can be lived*, because the Christian has the Spirit, and because God's love never changes (viii.).

(*d*) *The problem of unbelieving Israel* (ix.–xi.).

(1) God has the *right* to reject Israel if He will (ix.).

(2) By their unbelief they *deserve* to be rejected (x.).

(3) Yet *some* Jews believe, so that God has *not* rejected them *as a nation* (xi. 1–6).

(4) The *Gentiles* have been brought in (xi. 7–12).

(5) Israel will also *turn to Christ* some day (xi. 13–36).

II. *The Christian Life in Practice* (xii. 1–xv. 13).

(*a*) *The consecrated life described* (xii.).

(*b*) *Particular duties* (xiii. 1–xv. 13).

(1) *Obedience to the Government* (xiii. 1–7).

(2) *Honesty and love* (xiii. 8–14).

(3) *Consideration* for the weak brother (xiv. 1–xv. 13).

Conclusion (xv. 14–xvi. 27).

1. His missionary *labours*, and *plans* for the future (xv. 14–33).
2. *Greetings* to friends at Rome (xvi. 1–23).
3. *Doxology* (xvi. 25–27).

CHAPTER XIV

The Epistles of the Imprisonment: Ephesians, Colossians, Philemon, Philippians

We come now to a group of Epistles, closely connected together and containing some of Paul's profoundest teaching.

Prison letters.—These four letters were certainly written during one of Paul's imprisonments, for he refers in each of them to his position as a prisoner:

Eph. iii. 1: I Paul, the *prisoner* of Christ Jesus in behalf of you Gentiles.

Col. iv. 3: The mystery of Christ, for which I am also *in bonds*.

Phil. i. 13: So that *my bonds* became manifest in Christ throughout the whole prætorian guard.

Philemon 1.: Paul, a *prisoner* of Christ Jesus.

Cæsarea or Rome?—Until recently it has always been assumed that they must have been written during either the two years spent at Rome (Acts xxviii. 30) or the two years spent at Cæsarea (Acts xxiv. 27). If these are the only possible alternatives, there is very little doubt that they belong to *the First Roman Imprisonment*.

1. Eph. vi. 19, 20, Phil. i. 13, and Col. iv. 3, 4 imply that he was free to preach and teach. This was more likely to be the case at Rome, where he lived in "his own hired dwelling" (Acts xxviii. 30),

than at Cæsarea, where his confinement was more severe.

2. He was expecting to be released very shortly (Phil. ii. 23, 24). But at Cæsarea he was making up his mind to appeal to Rome and knew that he would not be free for a long while to come.

3. The gift from the Philippians for which he was very grateful (Phil. iv. 10, 14) would hardly be needed at Cæsarea, where he seems to have been in easy circumstances, see p. 113. But it would be very acceptable at Rome, where he may well have felt the expenses of the trial.

4. The runaway slave, Onesimus, who forms the subject of Philemon, would be more likely to try to hide himself in Rome than in Cæsarea.

5. The subjects treated in these Epistles are very different from those in the Romans group; and in some respects there is a development in Paul's thought which indicates the lapse of a considerable time after the writing of Romans.

Ephesus or Rome?—Another rather startling theory, first suggested about thirty years ago on the Continent, has been strongly advocated recently by Professor G. S. Duncan and some other British scholars: that these Epistles were written during an unmentioned imprisonment at *Ephesus* in the period covered by Acts xix.

1. *Was there an Ephesian imprisonment?* (1) In favour of it we have the following facts: (*a*) 2 Cor. xi. 23, 24 indicates that Paul suffered more persecutions than are described in Acts; (*b*) We gather from Rome. xvi. 3, 4 that there was some occasion

when Priscilla and Aquila saved his life at the peril of their own, and this may have been at Ephesus, for they settled there (Acts xviii. 18. 19); (*c*) 1 Cor. xv. 32, generally interpreted metaphorically, may mean that Paul was once in danger of having to face the lions in the arena at Ephesus.

(2) If we ask why there is no more definite reference to these perils in Acts, it is suggested that, seeing that Luke's purpose in writing was probably to win the protection of the Roman Government for Christianity, he would not feel himself under any obligation to describe events in which there had been rather serious trouble between the Christians and the Government.

We conclude, therefore, that it is not impossible that there may have been an imprisonment at Ephesus.

2. *Could the Epistles have been written then?* Professor Duncan's two main arguments are that: (1) Between them the Prison Epistles indicate at least ten journeys of friends from Philippi or Colossæ during the period of the writing of the letters, and the journey from either place to Rome would be very much more costly, both in time and money, then to Ephesus, and indeed might be prohibitively costly. (2) The runaway slave, Onesimus, would be more likely to seek hiding in Ephesus, less than a hundred miles away, than to go all the way to Rome.

These arguments seem to ignore the fact that Rome was the London of that day, and that there would be continual coming and going between all the great cities and Rome.

3. *The Epistle to the Philippians.* It is not at all easy to think that Paul is writing from Ephesus.

(1) The only passages that serve as clues both point more naturally to Rome than to Ephesus. (*a*) "My bonds in Christ became manifest throughout the whole prætorian guard" (Phil. i. 13). It is true that there was a *prætorium* in most of the larger cities, as a name for either a barracks, or the troops quartered there, or the residence of the governor; but, in the absence of any hint to the contrary, it is natural to think of the "prætorium" at *Rome.* It may be noted that in Acts xxviii. 16 (R.V. margin) describing Paul's arrival in Rome some MSS. add: "The centurion delivered the prisoners to the captain of the prætorian guard." (*b*) In Phil. iv. 22 "Those of Cæsar's household" naturally suggests Christian slaves attached to the Emperor's palace in *Rome*, but, if Paul was writing from Ephesus, it must mean merely "slaves of the Emperor." No doubt there were some of these at Ephesus, but we should expect some hint somewhere in the Epistle that Paul means Ephesus, not Rome.

(2) His sublime hope in death (Phil. i. 21, 23) seems to be a great advance on the expectation in 1 Cor. xv. 31 that he and most of his readers would live to see the Return of Christ; yet on this theory 1 Corinthians was written within a few months of Philippians.

4. *The Epistles to the Ephesians, Colossians and Philemon.* There is no question that these three must be dated together. Clearly Philemon and Colossians were written together; and, if Ephesians

is the work of Paul, it must have been written at the same time as Colossians, for there are large sections in which one epistle is a duplicate of the other. Yet the difficulty of dating these three from Ephesus is even greater than in the case of Philippians, so much so that some who accept the theory for Philippians reject it for the others.

It must not be supposed, however, that the title "Ephesians" necessarily rules out Ephesus as the place of origin, for in our earliest copies of Eph. i. 1, the words "at Ephesus" are left blank, and this Epistle was almost certainly a circular letter to the numerous Churches in the Roman provinces of "Asia." The real difficulties are that:

(1) Ephesians and Colossians indicate a stage of thought for which any Ephesian imprisonment would be much too early, especially the reference to "the Colossian heresy," and the very mature conception of the Church as the mystic "Bride of Christ."

(2) This dating would mean that the two years of imprisonment at Rome, in which Paul had considerable freedom of action (Acts xxviii. 30), passed without producing any writing of his that has survived. This seems so difficult to believe as to be almost incredible.

To sum up, there is no clear and indisputable evidence that there was any Ephesian imprisonment at all, and the general character of the Epistles fits in much more naturally with Rome as the place of origin than Ephesus. Even in the case of Philippians, for which an Ephesian origin seems less impossible than for the other three, it can only be maintained by some straining of such clues as there are. We shall, therefore, follow the familiar course, and treat all four as having been written towards the end of thc First Roman Imprisonment, about A.D. 62.

Paul's life as a prisoner.—We see from Acts xxviii. 30, 31 that Paul was allowed considerable freedom, and lived in his own house with one soldier to guard him. Most of the regiment would take this duty in turn, so that he was able in course of time to speak of Christ to almost the whole prætorian guard (Phil. i. 13).

Luke had accompanied him to Rome, and Timothy must also have been with him, for he is included in the salutations in Phil. i. 1, Col. i. 1 and Philemon 1. Other friends mentioned in these Epistles are Mark, Aristarchus and Demas (Philemon 24) and Justus (Col. iv. 11), whilst Tychicus was also available to act as Paul's messenger (Col. iv. 7).

Three interesting events came to break the monotony of this period, and led to the writing of these letters:

1. *Onesimus*, a slave belonging to a Colossian friend of Paul's, Philemon, had robbed his master and made his way to Rome. In some way not described he was brought to Paul and was converted, and Paul became very much attached to him.

2. *Epaphras*, the founder of the Church at Colossæ, arrived with news of a serious outbreak of heresy in the Church there through the influence of a new teacher who had come to the place, and who is referred to, but not named, in Col. ii. 8, 16, 18.

Paul at once wrote the Epistle to the *Colossians*, and despatched it by Tychicus (Col. iv. 7); for Epaphras seems to have been arrested and detained in Rome as a prisoner (Philemon 23).

Paul took advantage of this opportunity to persuade Onesimus to return to his master, and wrote the Epistle to *Philemon*, urging him to receive the fugitive kindly. To encourage and help Onesimus he also commended him to the Colossian Church, of which he would now become a member (Col. iv. 9).

As Tychicus also carried the Epistle to the *Ephesians* (Eph. vi. 21), it is clear that this letter was written at the same time.

3. *Epaphroditus* arrived from Philippi, bringing a gift from the Church there. Unfortunately, he fell ill in Rome, and Paul had a time of some anxiety concerning him (Phil. ii. 25–27). But in the end he recovered, and was able to carry back Paul's letter of thanks, the Epistle to the *Philippians*.

A.—THE EPISTLE TO THE EPHESIANS

1. *To whom was it addressed?*

It is quite clear that Ephesians was written at the same time as Colossians, but there is great uncertainty as to the Church to which it was addressed.

(*a*) Paul had spent two years at Ephesus, and had also met the Ephesian elders afterwards (Acts xx. 16, 17), yet there are *no personal references or greetings*: no name is mentioned except that of Tychicus, his messenger, and there is no reference whatever to Paul's experiences during his stay among them.

(*b*) *The teaching is very general.* There is no hint of any difficulty connected with the Church at Ephesus in particular, and there is not a line of the teaching which would not apply equally well to *any* Church.

(*c*) The great MSS., א and B, omit the words "at Ephesus" in chapter i. 1, and perhaps meant the address to be left blank: "To the saints that are in——" In that case the name of the particular Church could be filled in as it was read.

These facts make it almost certain that Ephesians was a *circular letter* to the Churches of the province of Asia, to be read to each of them in turn. Probably Ephesus, as the largest of these Churches and the one that Tychicus would reach first, retained the original letter, whilst the others contented themselves with copies. Apparently the copy Marcion knew of was that which went to Laodicea, for he calls it the "Epistle to the *Laodiceans*." Unless we are to suppose that another letter of Paul has been lost, Paul must have meant by "the epistle from Laodicea" in Col. iv. 16 our Ephesians, which would be passed on to Colossæ from Laodicea if we are right in regarding it as a circular letter.

2. *By whom was it written?*

The Pauline authorship of Ephesians is not so generally admitted as that of most of his other Epistles. The early testimony is quite satisfactory: it is quoted as Paul's very early, and may even have been used by Peter. Yet there are some marked differences in style, including some Hebrew constructions, from which the Greek of Paul is singularly free. The chief differences is that the sentences are very much longer and more involved than is customary with Paul, e.g., the R.V. shows that chapter i. 3–14 is *one* sentence and verses 15–23 another! Dr. J. H. Moulton suggested that the difference might be explained if we suppose that whilst Paul was writing to the Colossians he instructed one of his companions, such as Timothy, to draft a letter for the other Churches of that neighbourhood on much the same lines as Colossians, except for the references to the particular heresy at Colossæ, and that he then *revised* it himself and *sent* it in his own name. This would account for the numerous resemblances to Colossians (see pp. 175, 176), and would explain how it is that the style of some parts seems so unlike that of Paul.

3. *The teaching of Ephesians*

This Epistle is remarkable for the depth and fullness of its teaching on two doctrines:

The Nature of Christ.—The greatness and mystery of Christ's Person. A whole book would hardly suffice to expound chapter i. Paul seems to be overwhelmed with the wonder of Redemption and the mystery of God's purpose, which goes *back* to all eternity. He also sees this purpose reaching *forward* into eternity, and struggles to describe the end of God's great design, when all things shall be gathered into one in Christ (i. 10).

The Church.—The second topic which distinguishes this Epistle is its teaching on *the Church, its relation to Christ, and the meaning of Church membership.*

In the earlier Epistles Paul seems to think chiefly of the various Churches in different localities, each of them largely independent of the rest. But here there emerges the thought of *the* Church as a great, invisible, spiritual community, which embraces all the local Churches and all believers, recognized or unrecognized, past, present or to come.

He describes the Church under two great figures:

(*a*) It is the *Body* of which Christ is the *Head*. The various Churches and their members are the limbs of this Body, and each part has its own work to do in the life of the whole (iv. 1–16).

(*b*) It is the *Bride of Christ*, the object of His special love, and, so to speak, His second self, without which He is incomplete (v. 22–33).

The Christian's walk.—In the *practical section* of the Epistle the most interesting feature is the description of the Christian's manner of life as a *walk*:

iv. 1: To walk worthily of the calling wherewith ye were called.

iv. 17: That ye no longer walk as the Gentiles also walk.

v. 2: Walk in love.

v. 8: Walk as children of light.

OUTLINE OF EPHESIANS

Greeting (i. 1, 2).

I.—*Doctrinal Section* (i–iii).

1. *The sublime dignity and glory of Christ* as the *Redeemer* of the world, and the *gathering point* of the universe (i.).
2. *The greatness of their position* as Christians and children of God (ii.)
3. *The greatness of his position* as a preacher of the Gospel (iii.).

II.—*Practical Exhortations* (iv.–vi.).

They must "*walk worthily of their calling*":

1. *As members of Christ's Body, the Church* (iv. 1–16).
2. *As new men* putting away their old sins (iv. 17–32).
3. *As children of God* imitating their Father (v. 1–6).
4. *As children of light*, whether they are *husbands* or *wives*, *parents* or *children*, *masters* or *servants* (v. 7–vi. 9).
5. *As soldiers of Christ*, needing the whole armour of God (vi. 10–20).

Conclusion and *Benediction* (vi. 21–24).

B.—THE EPISTLE TO THE COLOSSIANS

1. *The Church at Colossæ*

Colossæ.—Colossæ lay about a hundred miles inland from Ephesus. At the time he wrote Paul had not visited the Church there (ii. 1), but he perhaps did so after his release. This was not one of the seven Churches of Asia mentioned in Rev. i. 11, though it was closely associated with them. These Churches were probably founded from Ephesus by friends and helpers of Paul either during or shortly after his two years' stay there. The R.V. of Col. i. 7 makes it clear that the Colossians learnt the Gospel from Epaphras, and that Paul regarded him as his substitute in this piece of missionary work, for he calls him "a faithful minister of Christ *on our behalf*," i.e., in my place.

The Epistle.—We have seen on p. 168 that the Epistle was written from Rome, because Epaphras was unable to cope with the heresy at Colossæ. It was despatched by Tychicus, because Epaphras was detained in Rome as a prisoner (Philemon 23).

2. *The heresy at Colossæ and Paul's reply*

Although the name of the false teacher is not given, we gather that he was a wordy, bombastic man, who made a show of philosophy (ii. 8). To judge from Paul's reply in the Epistle, the heresy had three characteristics:

(1) *View of Christ.—A defective theory of Christ's Nature.* There grew up within the next century a system of religious thought called *Gnosticism.* This took a number of different forms, and there were many attempts to combine it with the Christian belief. The leading idea was that there is a great series of beings, one above the other, reaching from man up to God, called "angels," "powers," "words," etc. The mention of thrones, dominions principalities, and powers in chapter i. 16 and the reference to the worshipping of angels in chapter ii. 18, show that the heresy at Colossæ was a crude form of this theory. That is to say, Christ was regarded as one of the most exalted of these beings, but not as God.

Paul replies by laying great stress on the *full divinity of Christ*: He is "the image of the invisible God, the first-born of all creation" (i. 15); He is to have "the pre-eminence" in all things (i. 18); "all the fullness of God" dwells in Him (i. 19 and ii. 9); and in Him "all the treasures of wisdom and knowledge are hidden" (ii. 3).

(2). *Ritualism.*—The teacher also laid great stress

on *religious ceremonial*, such as the observance of many sacred days and the worshipping of angels (ii. 16, 18).

Paul replies by reminding the Colossians that Christ had proved a complete and sufficient Saviour to them (ii. 10), and that they had found in Him both forgiveness and new life (ii. 13). What can circumcision or other mere ceremonies do for them, seeing that Christ has circumcised them inwardly in their hearts (ii. 11)?

(3) *Ascetic rules.*—The false teacher, advocated *an austere, ascetic life as necessary to holiness.* He laid down strict rules about food and drink (ii. 16); and this, that, and the other thing were not to be touched or tasted or handled (ii. 20–22). That is, he insisted on a severe, narrow, monkish type of life. This part of his teaching was probably derived from the *Essenes*, a gloomy, fanatical sect of Jews, who lived lives of great severity in our Saviour's day, many of them in lonely caves near the Dead Sea.

Paul denounces all such rules as useless: they are only man-made and do not touch our sinful nature (ii. 20–23). Real goodness does not consist in starving or torturing one's body, but in starving the sinful desires (iii. 5); not in abstaining from perfectly innocent things, but in abstaining from anger, malice, lying and the like (iii. 8, 9).

3. *Parallels between Colossians and Ephesians*

We have seen that these two Epistles were written at the same time and carried by the same messenger. This view is confirmed by the extraordinary number of parallels between them. Col. i. 15–29 treats more briefly all the three subjects found in Eph. i.–iii., and Col. iii. 18–iv. 1 is simple Eph. v. 22–vi. 9 a little abridged. Other parallels are Col. i. 14 and Eph. i. 7; Col. i. 24 and Eph. iv. 12; Col. ii. 13 and Eph. ii. 1, 5; Col. iii. 10 and Eph. iv. 24; Col. iii 16 and Eph. v. 19, 20; Col. iv. 7, 8 and Eph. vi. 21, 22.

OUTLINE OF COLOSSIANS

Introduction (i. 1–14).

Salutation (i. 1, 2), *Thanksgiving* (i. 3–8), *Prayer* (i. 9–14).

I.—*Paul's doctrine stated* (i. 15–29).

(*a*) *Christ's fitness to be the Saviour* as the Eternal Son of God (i. 15–20).

(*b*) *The reality of His salvation*, as they experienced it (i. 20–23).

(*c*) *The work of the true minister of Christ* (as distinguished from the false teacher) (i. 24–29).

II.—*His reply to the heretical teaching* (ii).

(*a*) He is *very anxious* about them (ii. 1–7).

(*b*) Christ has been *a full and complete Saviour* to them (ii. 8–15).

(*c*) Jewish ceremonial has *no meaning* for those who have known Christ's work in their hearts (ii. 10, 11, 16–19).

(*d*) *Ascetic rules* do not destroy *sinful desires* (ii. 20–23).

III.—*The life of the true Christian* (iii. 1–iv. 6).

A new life in union with Christ involves:

(*a*) *Putting away sin of every kind* (iii. 1–11).

(*b*) *Putting on holiness of every kind* (iii. 12–

iv. 1), both in the Church (iii. 16), and at home, as husbands or wives, parents or children, masters or servants (iii. 17–iv. 1).

(*c*) *Prayerfulness* (iv. 2–4).

(*d*) *Caution* in their behaviour and speech in the world (iv. 5, 6).

Conculsion (iv. 7–18).

(*a*) *Personal references:* Tychicus, Onesimus, and the friends at Rome (iv. 7–14).

(*b*) *Farewell* to the Church and *encouragement* to their minister, Archippus (iv. 15–17).

(*c*) *Benediction* (iv. 18).

C.—THE EPISTLE TO PHILEMON

1. *Philemon and Onesimus*

Philemon was a well-to-do gentleman of Colossæ and a leading member of the Church there, for the services were held in his house (v. 2). Apphia was his wife, and Archippus was either his son or brother, and appears to have been acting as minister of the Church, at least during the absence of Epaphras (Col. iv. 17). Philemon owed his conversion to Paul (*v.* 19), probably at the time of some visit to Ephesus whilst Paul was there.

Onesimus was his slave, and his name, which meant "profitable" or "helpful," was often given to slaves. He proved decidedly "unprofitable" (*v.* 11), for he absconded with money (*v.* 18). After his flight to Rome he was converted under the teaching of Paul (*v.* 10), and became exceedingly dear to him, so that Paul calls him his "very heart" (*v.* 12, R.V.), and would have liked to keep him if

Philemon had been willing (*vv.* 13, 14). But it was his obvious duty to return first to his master, and, as he had the right to put him to death, Paul wrote this beautiful letter to plead for him.

2. *The letter*

Date.—It was written from Rome at the same time as Colossians, for in Col. iv. 9 he commends Onesimus kindly to the Church at Colossæ. Timothy, Aristarchus, Luke and Epaphras are mentioned in both letters, and each contains a greeting to Archippus. There is no reference to Philemon in Colossians, because Paul was writing to him separately.

Contents.—No letter more charming, tender, and persuasive can well be imagined, and Paul shows himself here a great Christian gentleman.

Beginning as usual with a greeting and thanksgiving (*vv.* 1–7), he continues:

"I might as a minister of Christ put it to you as a *duty*, but I prefer to make it a *request*, that you will receive this latest spiritual son of mine, Onesimus. He has been false to his name hitherto, but now he will be really *profitable*; indeed, he is so profitable to me that I could wish to keep him. He left you for a time, but now he will be yours *for ever*, for he is not simply a slave, but your *brother* in Christ for ever. If he has robbed you, I will make it good, though you cannot forget that *you owe me* your very soul. Please do not let me plead in vain. But I am sure that you will do even more than I ask."

Outcome.—Tradition says that the plea was entirely successful, and that Philemon not only received Onesimus kindly, but set him free, and that he ultimately became a prominent Christian leader as Bishop of Berœa or, perhaps, of Ephesus.

Details.—Two details should be noted: (1) Paul calls himself "the aged" (*v.* 9). He can hardly have been more than sixty; yet his life had been one of such unusual toil, exposure, suffering, and anxiety that he might really be worn out quite early. (2) He asks Philemon to secure him a lodging (*v.* 22), so that he must have been anticipating a very speedy release.

3. *Permanent teaching of Philemon*

The abiding value of this little letter consists in what it has to teach on the subject of slavery. Paul and other New Testament writers never raise the question whether it is right to own slaves. Universal release was at that time quite unthinkable, for in many cities the enormous majority of the population were slaves. Indeed, a single individual sometimes owned 50,000 of them, and if they had all been released at once their position as unemployed free-men would have been far worse than their condition as slaves. Hence the New Testament aimed rather to make the masters *good* masters, and the slaves *good* slaves, than to abolish slavery'

Yet, perhaps without recognizing all that his words implied, Paul gave the real death-blow to slavery in Christian lands in the words: "No longer as a *servant*, but . . . *a brother* beloved" (*v.* 16). A Christian owner must wish for the salvation of his slaves. But if they become Christians, they become his *brothers* in Christ. How can he continue to regard them as his slaves? It was many centuries before the Church realized all that these words imply, but that is the principle which has killed slavery wherever Christian civilization prevails.

D.—THE EPISTLE TO THE PHILIPPIANS

1. *Paul and the Philippian Church*

The Philippian Church was the first outcome of Paul's call to Macedonia and his first fruit in Europe. He would never forget the beating with rods and that strange night in the prison. But neither would he forget some of his converts there, such as the Philippian jailer and the gentle-hearted Lydia (Acts xvi. 11–40). And they did not forget him, for twice during the stay of little more than three weeks at Thessalonica they sent him gifts (Phil. iv. 16).

The Church was small and poor (2 Cor. viii. 2), yet it was not feeble. Lydia, who had the enterprise to come all the way from Thyatira to establish herself in business (Acts xvi. 14), must have been a woman of considerable energy and resource; and the jailer would be a sturdy type of member. Furthermore, Luke remained at Philippi, and would be a tower of strength to the Church. Paul must have passed through Philippi both coming and going on the Third Journey (Acts xx. 1 and 6); and though no account is given of his stay, this was the dearest to him of all his Churches, and he would be sure to remain a little while among them.

2. *Circumstances which led to the writing of Philippians*

Towards the end of the First Roman Imprisonment the Philippians sent Epaphroditus with a gift to Paul. The immediate purpose of the letter was to acknowledge this gift (iv. 10–19). The serious illness of Epaphroditus may have prevented Paul from writing for some weeks or even months, and when he wrote he was expecting a speedy release (ii. 24). As the same hope is expressed in Philemon 22, Philippians must have been written at very nearly the same time as Colossians, Philemon, and Ephesians.

3. *Contents of Philippians*

The *message of thanks* (iv. 10–19) was the "excuse" for writing, but Paul naturally added a great deal more. Yet the letter would have been worth its place in the New Testament if it had consisted of nothing but this passage, for no gift was ever more gracefully and courteously acknowledged. He welcomes the gift, yet he can do all things in Christ (*v.* 13), and could have done without it. He welcomes it chiefly because of the credit that it will add to their account in the books of God (*v.* 17). They have supplied *some* of his needs out of their poverty, and though he can make them no return, *God* will supply *all* their needs out of His unlimited wealth (*v.* 19).

Personal News.—This is much the *most intimate* of Paul's Epistles, and abounds in indications of his *affection* for the Philippians, such as those in chapters i. 7, 8 and iv. 1. He seeks to allay their fears concerning his fate: good has come of his imprisonment (i. 12), and he is quite prepared to lay down his life (i. 21–24), though he expects to be released (i. 25, ii. 24). He reassures them about their messenger, Epaphroditus (ii. 25–30).

His experience.—The Epistle is remarkable for the glimpses that it affords of Paul's *spiritual experience*—his confidence in the life beyond (i. 21, 23), the satisfaction he found in Christ (ii. 1), the "gain" which far outweighs any "loss" involved in becoming a Christian (iii. 4–11).

Christian ideals.—More than any Epistle, Philippians shows us *the ideal of the Christian life*. Its chief characteristics are (1) *high aspiration* (ii. 12–16 and iii. 12–14), and (2) *joy* (iii. 1 and iv. 4–7). It is extraordinary that under such conditions his heart seemed full of joy, for the words "joy" and "rejoice" occur again and again.

Warnings.—Even with so satisfactory a Church as this there were certain *warnings* that Paul needed to give. (1) The *Judaists* were still at work, and Paul feared their influence even at Philippi (iii. 1–8). (2) There was a certain amount of *quarrelling* in the Church, and in chapter ii. 1–4 Paul appeals to them to avoid it, whilst in chapter iv. 2, 3 he mentions specially the case of two women, Euodia and Syntyche, who seem to have had some difference.

Doctrine.—There is only one little section of *doctrine* (ii. 5–11), and that is introduced incidentally in appealing to them to consider one another, and imitate the self-forgetfulness of Christ. Yet it happens to be one of the most important passages in the New Testament on the subject of the *Nature of Christ and His Humiliation in becoming Man*.

OUTLINE OF PHILIPPIANS

This letter is so intimate and informal that it is not easy to analyse. There are *two parentheses*:

(*a*) chapter ii. 19–30, referring to Timothy and Epaphroditus; (*b*) chapter iv. 2, 3, referring to Euodia and Syntyche. The rest of the Epistle may then be outlined thus:

Introduction (i. 1–11).
(*a*) *Salutation* (i. 1, 2). (*b*) *Thanksgiving* (i. 3-8). (*c*) *Prayer* (i. 9–11).

I.—*News concerning himself* (i. 12–26).

II.—*His hopes concerning them* (i. 27–ii. 18).
(1) That they will *endure persecution faithfully* (i. 27–30).
(2) That they will be *united* (ii. 1–11).
(3) That their lives will be *progressive* (ii. 12–18).

III.—*Warnings* (iii. 1–iv. 1).
(1) Against the *Judaists* (iii. 1–11).
(2) Against *relaxation* of effort (iii. 12–iv. 1).

IV.—*Exhortations* (iv. 4–9).
(1) To *rejoice* in Christ (iv. 4–7).
(2) To seek a *full and rounded* character (iv. 8, 9).

V.—*Thanks for their gift* (iv. 10–19).

Conclusion (iv. 20–23).
(1) *Doxology* (iv. 20).
(2) *Greetings* (iv. 21, 22).
(3) *Benediction* (iv. 23).

CHAPTER XV

The Pastoral Epistles:

1 Timothy, Titus, and 2 Timothy

The Name.—These are called the *Pastoral Epistles* because they were written to Paul's younger colleagues, Timothy and Titus, to guide and encourage them in their work as pastors or ministers. But they also touch on many subjects connected with *the life of the Church*, and by using the plural "you" instead of the singular "thee," e.g., in Titus iii. 15, Paul shows that he thought it possible that at least parts of them might be read to the Churches of which Timothy and Titus had charge.

A.—WERE THEY WRITTEN BY PAUL?

The genuineness of these Epistles is much more seriously questioned than that of Paul's other writings, and must be considered in some detail.

External evidence.—The testimony of early Christian writers, or the *external evidence*, is quite satisfactory.

It is true that they are not quoted as the work of Paul before Irenæus, A.D. 185, but there are clear echoes of them in Polycarp about A.D. 100, though he does not happen to mention Paul as the writer.

The authorship does not appear to have been questioned till A.D. 400 or later.

Modern objections and replies to them

Rather serious objections are raised to-day, and the most important of them must be noted.

1. *History. Some deny that Paul was released after his First Roman Imprisonment, but if he was not released he cannot have written these Epistles.*

All these Epistles imply that Paul was released and arrested again some four or five years later, and that he wrote them in that interval.

(*a*) In 1 Tim. i. 3, 4, Paul says that when he was going into Macedonia he bade Timothy remain at Ephesus, and that he wishes him to do so still. Now the last journey into Macedonia mentioned in Acts is that in Acts xx. 1–3. But on that occasion Timothy left Ephesus with Paul, for he was with him at Corinth when he wrote Romans (see Rom. xvi. 21).

(*b*) Titus i. 5 implies that Paul had been to Crete and had left Titus there. But Acts mentions no mission of either Paul or Titus in Crete.

(*c*) According to 2 Timothy, Paul is in Rome and begs Timothy to come to him (2 Tim. iv. 9). But in the First Imprisonment Timothy was with him, for he joined in the greetings in Phil. i. 1, Col. i. 1, and Philemon 1. Also Paul knew that he would be condemned at his next appearance before Nero and that he must die very shortly (2 Tim. iv. 16, 17, and 6–8). But in the First Imprisonment he was quite confident of a speedy release (Phil. ii. 23, 24).

Hence these Epistles can only be genuine if Paul was released at the close of the imprisonment described in Acts xxviii. 30, and made a final missionary tour in which he visited Crete, Ephesus, and Macedonia.

Was Paul released?—There is nothing to contradict the belief that he was released. Acts xx. 38 says that he did not expect to see the Ephesians again, but many have lived to see their friends again long after bidding them a last farewell. Clement, Bishop of Rome (A.D. 95–100), states that Paul went to "the furthest limits of the West," so that he believed not only that he was released, but that his final tour included *Spain*. Some even of those who doubt whether Paul wrote these Epistles admit that he was released, and that he had some four or five years of liberty before his final arrest and martyrdom.

2. *Subjects*. The second objection raised against these Epistles is that *the subjects discussed are different from those treated in Paul's other Epistles, and they are not the kind of subjects in which we should expect him to feel an interest*. He has a great deal to say here about the Church and its *organization*, about Church *officers* and their appointment, and about *orthodox belief* and the danger of *heresy*. It is said that this is not like Paul, and that he cared more about evangelistic work than about Church arrangements, and more about faith in Christ than about orthodox belief.

To this we reply that:

(*a*) *Though these subjects are not prominent in the other Epistles, he has something to say about each of them*, e.g., 1 Cor. xii.–xiv. and Eph. iv. 1–16 deal with the Church and its officers; and Eph. i. and Col. i. and ii. both deal with questions of creed.

(*b*) *As his own end drew near he would feel the necessity of providing for these matters*, just as Wesley at the close of his life felt that, if the work of Methodism was to continue, it must be organized on right lines and must have a standard of doctrine.

(*c*) *The contents of these Epistles do not imply any date later than Paul's own lifetime.* His experience at Corinth a dozen years earlier must have warned him of the need of effective Church government and the danger that might arise from the appointment of unsuitable officers. Nor does the heresy he fears involve a long period of development. He had had to deal with the false teaching at Colossæ in A.D. 62; and if the Epistle of Jude is genuine, it it clear that heresy of the most blasphemous type developed in some localities within a few years of Paul's death.

(*d*) *There are many small details of which no forger would think*, e.g., "Let no man despise thy youth" (1 Tim. iv. 12), for though Timothy would be thirty-five to forty, he would still seem very young to Paul; the references to Timothy's childhood (2 Tim. i. 5) and to the persecution at Antioch, Iconium, and Lystra (2 Tim. iii. 11); and the mention of the cloak, books, and parchments left at Troas (2 Tim. iv. 13).

3. *Style and language.* The third objection raised is that *the style is different from that of Paul's other Epistles, and he uses many words not found in them.* Lists of the words found in the Pastorals only have

been compiled, and there are certainly many of them. Further, a few words are used in a new sense, e.g., the word "faith," which in Paul's other Epistles means the act of believing, is used here for the thing believed, "the Faith," or creed (1 Tim. iv. 1, etc.).

The *reply* to this objection is that:

(*a*) *The general style is different because Paul had aged very much in these few years:* we can hardly be surprised if he has lost some of his force and fire.

(*b*) *New words* are used because he is dealing with *new subjects*. It has been argued by W. P. Workman that in his later plays Shakespeare used just as high a proportion of new words as we find in these Epistles, though the force of this argument has been rather weakened by P. N. Harrison in his *Problem of the Pastoral Epistles*.

(*c*) The later meaning of the word "faith" is very nearly reached in 1 Cor. xvi. 13 and 2 Cor xiii. 5.

Conclusion. These Epistles claim to be by Paul, and the Early Church believed that they were by him. Those who reject them have to prove that they cannot have been written by him. None of the objections raised *prove* this, and we therefore have the right to believe that they were written by Paul.

Failing this, the most probable view is that they are manuals of Church administration and order drawn up by members of the Pauline circle and cast in the form of letters. They incorporate the substance of talks Paul had given on the Church and the work of the Ministry and fragments from letters he had written to his two most trusty lieutenants, Timothy and Titus.

B.—THE FIRST EPISTLE TO TIMOTHY

1. *Life of Timothy*

Timothy was the son of a Greek father and a Jewish mother (Acts xvi. 1). Apparently both the mother, Eunice, and the grandmother, Lois, were Christians (2 Tim. i. 5). Presumably both they and Timothy himself were converted on Paul's first visit to Lystra (or possibly Derbe) where they lived (Acts xvi. 1). Timothy would therefore remember the stoning of Paul at Lystra (Acts xiv. 19 and 2 Tim. iii. 11).

When Paul arrived the second time without either Barnabas or Mark he was attracted to Timothy as a suitable companion and helper. As he was of Jewish blood on one side, Paul circumcised him (Acts xvi. 3), in order that he might be the more free to work among any Jews whom they might meet. [Note that it was only the circumcision of *Gentile* converts that Paul objected to, and, quite consistently, he appears to have refused to allow Titus, a Greek, to be circumcised (Gal. ii. 3).]

Henceforth Timothy accompanied him on his journeys. He was not imprisoned at Philippi, and he and Silas were left in Berea when Paul went on to Athens (Acts xvii. 14). He also went back to see how the Church at Thessalonica was faring before he came on to Corinth to join Paul (i Thess. iii. 5, 6). Paul used him repeatedly on these small commissions. He accompanied him on the voyage to Rome, and his name appears in the salutations in Col. i. 1, Philemon 1, and Phil. i. 1.

From 1 Tim. i. 1. it is clear that on his final tour after his release Paul visited Ephesus once more, and left Timothy in charge there. He remained there until after Paul's final arrest, when Paul begged him to come to him in Rome just before the end (2 Tim. iv. 9). As Heb. xiii. 23 speaks of Timothy's being "set at liberty," it is probable that he suffered a short imprisonment at Rome at this time.

2. *Circumstances which led to the writing of the Epistle*

Timothy appears to have been in rather poor health (1 Tim. v. 23) and a little timid and weak in character, for in 1 Cor. xvi. 10, 11 Paul is evidently afraid that he may be nervous in dealing with the Corinthians. Some of the exhortations in 1 and 2 Timothy also suggest that Paul was not without fear that he might be carried away by false doctrine, and even by "youthful lusts" (2 Tim. ii. 22). This letter is written chiefly to encourage him to assert himself boldly as minister and leader of the Church (1 Tim. iv. 12), and to play his part loyally and manfully.

OUTLINE OF 1 TIMOTHY

Greeting (i. 1, 2).

I.—*Timothy's responsibility as a minister* (i. 3–20).
- (*a*) There is much false teaching (i. 3–11).
- (*b*) Salvation through Christ is the central thing to be preached (i. 12–20).

II.—*Instructions for the government of the Church* (ii. 1–iv. 5).

(*a*) How public prayer should be conducted (ii.).

(*b*) How ministers and officers should be chosen (iii. 1–13).

(*c*) The Church must be kept pure and loyal to the truth (iii. 14–iv. 5).

III.—*Personal advice to Timothy* (iv. 6–vi. 16).

(*a*) His personal life, studies, etc. (iv. 6–16).

(*b*) How he should deal with various classes: men, women, widows, presbyters, slaves (v. i–vi. 2).

(*c*) Solemn appeal to avoid the false teaching (vi. 3–16).

Conclusion (vi. 17–21).

C.—THE EPISTLE TO TITUS

1. *Life of Titus*

From Gal. ii. 1 it appears that Titus was a member of the Church at Antioch, and went with Paul to the Council of Jerusalem as a representative of that Church. He was a Gentile (Gal. ii. 3), and was probably a convert of Paul's, for he calls him his "true child" (Titus i. 4). There is some reason to think that he was Luke's brother.

Pressure was used at Jerusalem to compel him to be circumcised. Gal ii. 3 almost certainly means that Paul successfully resisted this, and that he was not circumcised.

He is comparatively little mentioned in Acts, but was Paul's messenger to Corinth during the crisis there (2 Cor. viii. 16, 17 and pp. 130, 138); and he was evidently a man of considerable strength, to whom Paul was able to entrust tasks of some difficulty.

After Paul's release Titus shared in the mission to Crete, and was left in charge there. This letter consists of advice on the management of the work. Some of the members had evidently been giving trouble, and one in particular Paul advises Titus to expel from the Church (iii. 10, 11).

OUTLINE OF TITUS

Greeting.

I.—*The type of officer that Titus should appoint* (i. 5–16).

Men of high moral character, and not the disloyal, money-seeking, or inconsistent.

II.—*The type of Christian character he is to set forth* (ii. 1–iii. 8).

(1) How Christians should live among themselves (ii.).

(2) How they should live in the world (iii. 1–8).

III.—*Personal advice to Titus* (iii. 9–11).

Conclusion (iii. 12–15).

D.—THE SECOND EPISTLE TO TIMOTHY

1. *Circumstances which led to the writing of 2 Timothy*

This is the last of Paul's writings. He is now in prison awaiting sentence and death (iv. 6), and begs Timothy to come with all speed (iv. 9) and to bring Mark with him (iv. 11). Timothy was still at Ephesus, and Paul wishes him to finish his ministry there well. Further, the journey to Rome was somewhat perilous; indeed, it appears to have involved Timothy in imprisonment (Heb. xiii. 23). Hence the Epistle is partly given to stirring up his rather feeble courage. As he will have to come through Troas, Paul asks him to bring certain things he had left there—a cloak and some books and parchments, the last being presumably rolls of Scripture. Thus almost the last words Paul wrote show his unabated interest in study and his undying love for the Bible.

OUTLINE OF 2 TIMOTHY

Introduction (i. 1–5).

I.—*Exhortation to a faithful and courageous ministry* (i. 6–ii. 13).

II.—*Exhortation to sound doctrine*, avoiding foolish discussions and false teaching (ii. 14–iii. 9).

III.—*Exhortation to loyalty* (iii. 10–iv. 8).

(1) He has shared persecution with Paul before (iii. 10–13).

(2) He has been taught the truth from infancy and must not forsake it now (iii. 14–17).

(3) Opposition will tend to grow worse (iv. 1–5).

(4) Paul himself will soon be passing away (iv. 6–8).

IV.—*Personal news, requests, and greetings* (iv. 9–21).

Benediction (iv. 22).

CHAPTER XVI

The Epistle to the Hebrews

This great and precious book tells us neither *to* whom, nor *by* whom, nor *when*, nor *why* it was written; and it is probably impossible to reach an absolutely certain conclusion on any of these points. If we could only make sure of any one of them it would be easier to decide the rest.

A.—TO WHOM WAS IT WRITTEN?

The readers addressed.—There is no opening salutation or address: the title "To (the) Hebrews" was given to the Epistle not by the writer, but by the Early Church. A number of continental scholars and a few British ones, including Moffatt and Scott, argue for *Gentile* readers. But the whole character of the Epistle, abounding in Old Testament quotations and references to Jewish worship and sacrifices, suggests very strongly that its first readers must have been *Jews* by birth and training. It is clear, however, that, if they were Jews, they were *Christian* Jews.

But "Christian Jews" is very vague. Can we know more?

(*a*) The readers were *Greek-speaking Jews*, often called *Hellenists* or *Grecians* (see Acts vi. 1), for the Epistle was written in Greek, and the Old Testament quotations are taken not from the Hebrew, but from the Septuagint, i.e., the Greek version of the Old Testament.

(*b*) They were *some definite group* of Hellenists, for they knew the writer and Timothy, and certain Christians belonging to Italy (xiii. 23, 24).

(*c*) *They had not seen Jesus*, but had heard the Gospel from some of the *Apostles* (ii. 3).

(*d*) They had been Christians *for a long while* at the time the Epistle was written (v. 12 and xiii. 7, the latter passage implying that their original teachers were dead—see R.V.).

Where?—Such a group might probably be found in almost any of the towns where the Christians were numerous enough to form more than one congregation, for in such a case the Greek-speaking Jewish Christians would almost certainly make up a separate House-Church. The places suggested are:

(*a*) *Jerusalem*. But there many of the members would have seen Jesus.

(*b*) *Alexandria*. But there Timothy was not likely to be known, and chapter xiii. 23 would have no interest.

(*c*) *Antioch* and (*d*) *Cæsarea* would both suit well if it was written *from* Rome.

(*e*) *Rome*. Many now favour Rome, because the earliest traces of the use of the Epistle are found in Roman writers. "They from Italy" (xiii. 24) would then be Italian Christians living where the Epistle was written, who send greetings to their old Roman friends. The chief difficulty is that it has generally been supposed that Timothy was imprisoned at Rome after going there to join Paul (2 Tim. iv. 9), in which case the mention of his release would imply that the Epistle was written *at* Rome. But it is possible that he was imprisoned elsewhere.

B.—BY WHOM WAS IT WRITTEN?

Paul?—The Epistle does not name its writer, so that we have to be guided entirely by the evidence. The practically universal opinion is that *whoever wrote it, Paul did not.*

(*a*) *External evidence.*

(1) The R.V. calls it the "Epistle of Paul," but only because the Revisers were not allowed to touch the titles, for the oldest MSS. call it simply "To Hebrews."

(2) The authorship was so doubtful that for a long time it was excluded from the Canon. But in the end its spiritual quality compelled the Church to recognize it as inspired and admit it. They seem then to have argued that, as it was inspired, it must have been written by one of the apostolic group; and since no one claimed it, it was put down to Paul.

(3) There was never any strong or general belief that Paul wrote it. In A.D. 345 Origen, who valued it very highly, said quite frankly that who wrote it God only knows certainly.

(*b*) *Internal evidence.*

(1) Paul's name is never mentioned in the Epistle, though every known letter of his begins, "Paul, an Apostle," etc.

(2) The writer had not seen Jesus (ii. 3), but

Paul always insisted most earnestly that *he had* seen the Lord (1 Cor. ix. 1 and xv. 8).

(3) The Old Testament quotations are from the Septuagint, but Paul often shows that he was familiar with the Hebrew.

(4) The style is smooth and polished with none of Paul's excitement and broken, disjointed sentences. His most characteristic words and phrases are missing, e.g., he never speaks of "Jesus" as this writer does, but always calls Him "the Lord," or "Christ," or "Christ Jesus," or "Christ Jesus our Lord."

(5) The great truths of the Gospel are stated in quite a different way from Paul's. [There is, however, no contradiction of Paul's doctrine; indeed, the writer seems to have had Paul's teaching at the back of his mind, and perhaps used some of his Epistles.]

It is not too much to say, therefore, that *the whole weight of both the external and the internal evidence is against the Pauline authorship.*

Possible Authors.—Many possible writers have been suggested:

(1) *Silas.* A mere guess, with nothing to support it.

(2) *Luke.* Some parts resemble Acts in style, but Luke was a Gentile, knowing little of Jewish ritual and little interested in it.

(3) *Barnabas.* A Greek-speaking Jew from Cyprus, a companion of Paul, and a Levite, well acquainted with the Jewish services.

(4) *Apollos.* A Greek-speaking Jew, with the

philosophic ideas characteristic of Alexandria, "mighty in the Scriptures," and familiar with Paul's teaching. His painful recollections of the Apollos-party at Corinth (1 Cor. i. 12) would incline him to conceal his name, as he would have no wish to give rise to another party.

In the *Expository Times*, Nov., 1922, Professor Vernon Bartlet has made a strong case for Apollos. He finds indications in the Epistle that the readers were a section of the Jewish Christians in the Christian Church of some foreign city, wealthy, cultured and fit to be teachers, but holding aloof from the rank and file. The recent martyrdom of Paul had utterly discouraged them, and they were in danger of abandoning Christianity. Such a group was likely to exist at *Ephesus*. If so, *Apollos* would have influence with them (Acts xviii. 24, etc.); and his Alexandrian training would account for the style and the special way in which the writer uses the Old Testament. His companionship with Paul would also account for Pauline ideas in the Epistle. Timothy was also well known at Ephesus, and his release (xiii. 23) would be a great encouragement to the Church there, as proving that their enemies were not all-powerful. Professor Bartlet supposes that Apollos, whom Paul was expecting to join him at Nicopolis just before the final arrest (Tit. iii. 13), went with him as far as Rome and then returned. If he wrote the Epistle on his way home, say at Brindisi, it would be natural to send greetings from "those of *Italy*" rather than those "at Rome" (xiii. 24). The absence of author's name and greeting at the beginning he accounts for by supposing that the original direction to a small special group was removed to make the Epistle available for a wider circle.

(5) *Priscilla.* A brilliant suggestion, favoured by Peake and Moulton. She was probably capable of writing the book; the low estimate of women would compel her to conceal her name if the Epistle was to exert any influence; she would be interested in Jewish Christians; and if the Church addressed was at Rome, she and Aquila had been closely associated with it (Acts xviii. 2; Rom. xvi. 3).

Some also see a feminine touch in the reference to heroines of faith, Sarah (xi. 11), Rahab (xi. 31), and the women who received their dead raised to life again (xi. 35); but Rahab is also mentioned in James ii. 25, so that this argument will not carry much weight.

(6) *Joint authorship.* An ingenious suggestion was made by the late Rev. T. F. Lockyer. He supposed that Apollos and Paul planned the Epistle together. Apollos then wrote it, and sent it to Paul for revision shortly before his martyrdom. His death prevented his revising it; but Luke and Timothy, who were both at Rome at the time, undertook the task; and the finished Epistle was probably sent to Cæsarea, where Paul and Luke were well known. This theory has still to be worked out, but it would perhaps account for all the facts: (1) The smooth style and copious use of the Old Testament in the Septuagint form would be due to Apollos. (2) Luke's share in the work would

explain the presence of some of his words. (3) The origin in Rome would explain the reference to Timothy's release, if it was there that he was imprisoned (xiii. 23), and the greetings from the Christians of Italy (xiii. 24). (4) The joint authorship would explain the absence of the writer's name. (5) The slight connexion with Paul would explain the belief some had that he was the writer.

Date of Hebrews

Most of their first teachers had passed away (xiii. 7 R.V.). Even though the writer uses the word "Tabernacle," not "Temple," his continual references to Jewish services suggest that the Jewish system was still in full activity and that the Temple had not yet been destroyed. At the same time, the end of Judaism was evidently approaching (viii. 13). This points to a date shortly before the Fall of Jerusalem. The war which ended in the ruin of the city lasted from A.D. 66 to 70. Some such date as A.D. 67 would meet the case, and would suit any of the theories of authorship mentioned above.

Moffatt and others, however, who regard the Epistle as written for Gentile readers, connect it less closely with the Fall of Jerusalem and date it about A.D. 85.

C.—THE AIM OF HEBREWS

Warning.—The Epistle is *a most earnest exhortation to remain true to Christianity.* What was it that the writer feared?

If we are right in supposing that the readers were Jewish Christians, *two dangers* may have arisen:

(1) *Return to Judaism.*—The struggle of Jerusalem in its last days stirred the heart of every Jew to its very depths. The unbelieving Jews would most certainly say that it was the disloyalty of the Christian Jews to the religion of their fathers that was bringing ruin upon the nation. There would therefore be the *temptation to return to Judaism.* If this was the peril, the writer meets it by showing that to return would be gross disloyalty to Christ, and that they could not be disloyal to God in becoming Christians, because God had sent Jesus Christ to perfect and complete the old system.

(2) *Abandonment of Religion.*—Jewish Christians still used the Temple and its services in addition to attendance at the Christian meetings; and the old system was very precious to them. The ruin that was so obviously coming upon their nation made it seem as if God had forsaken His ancient people in their need. They may have been tempted to wonder whether they could trust Him to keep the promises of the New Covenant. There was thus a danger that *they might abandon religion altogether*, as many do under the influence of a great calamity. The writer meets this temptation by showing that:

(*a*) Christianity is the perfecting of Judaism, and all that was best in the old system will survive in the new.

(*b*) Judaism has served its purpose, so that God will not be unfaithful if He lets it perish now, and they too must consent to let it go.

(*c*) Their suffering and dismay are the chastening which God gives to His sons.

(*d*) The Old Covenant brought terrible penalties

on those who were unfaithful; the penalty for the apostate Christian is even more terrible.

D.—LEADING IDEAS OF HEBREWS

The supreme idea of Hebrews is that Christ and Christianity completely *fulfil* and *perfect* the Old Testament *prophecies* and the Old Testament *system.*

Jesus as Apostle.—Christ is God's last great Messenger to men: He is God's Son and His "express image," and is now at God's right hand (i. 3). He is thus greater than any of the *prophets* (i. 1, 2). But He is also greater than the *angels*, whom the Jews believed to have had some share in the giving of the Law (i. 4–ii. 4). Further, He is greater than *Moses*, who established the Old Covenant (iii.), and greater than *Joshua*, and can lead us into a better Promised Land (iv. 1–13).

Jesus as High Priest.—Jesus is the ideal High Priest, taking the place of all the Jewish priests and offering the last great Sacrifice. He has perfect sympathy because He became our Brother and was tempted (ii. 17, 18). He was appointed by God like *Aaron* (v. 4–7). But he has a greater priesthood than Aaron and his successors, for His is like *Melchizedek's* (v. 10). Aaron's line held their office by inheritance, not by any personal fitness, Melchizedek was chosen directly by God because of his *unique character*. He was not only a priest, but a *king* (vii. 1). We know nothing of his parentage, birth, or death, so that he became a type of the undying or *eternal* (vii. 3). And again, his priesthood was older and higher than Aaron's, because, when Abraham paid tithes to him, all his *descendants* virtually did so, including Aaron and all who succeeded him as high priest, (vii. 4–10). But if Christ's High-Priesthood is "after the order of Melchizedek" it, too, must be higher than that of Aaron in all these ways.

The New Covenant.—Christ has introduced a New Covenant (see Luke xxii. 20). This is superior to the Old, and must take its place. Earthly High Priests died, Christ is eternal; they were sinful, He is sinless; they could only present the blood of bulls and goats; He can present His own; they merely entered into the Holy of Holies once a year, He is always in the holiest of all, in God's very presence; their sacrifices could not take away sin, His can sanctify; their scarifices had to be repeated, His is offered once for all. These are the thoughts worked out in chapters viii. 1–x. 18.

Exhortations.—The Epistle is marked by several *warnings and exhortations* introduced at certain points in the argument, namely, chapters ii. 1–4, iii. 1–iv. 13 and v. 11–vi. 20. In the outline of the Epistle these should be regarded as parentheses. The concluding chapters, x. 19–xiii. 17, consist entirely of practical exhortations. Note the terrible warning against apostasy in chapter x. 26–31, very like that in chapter vi. 4–8, and the stirring words of encouragement based on the long list of heroes and heroines of faith in chapters xi. 1–xii. 4. The *concluding prayer* (xiii. 20, 21) is particularly beautiful.

OUTLINE OF HEBREWS

A.—Doctrine

I.—*Christ the Mediator of the New Covenant and our High Priest* (i.–vii.).

(*a*) *His fitness to be the ideal High Priest.*

(1) He is *God's Son*, greater than *prophets* (i. 1–3), or *angels* (i. 4–14).

(2) He is our *Brother*, *nearer* to us than angels (ii. 5–18).

(3) He is thus the *ideal High Priest* (iv. 14–16).

(*b*) *His appointment as High Priest.*

(1) He was appointed by God like *Aaron* (v. 1–10).

(2) He is *greater* than Aaron, for He resembles *Melchizedek*, who was *King* as well as *Priest* and was appointed by God's *oath* to an *undying* priesthood (vii.).

II.—*The New Covenant introduced by Christ* (viii. 1–x. 18).

(*a*) *It was needed because the Old was defective* (viii.).

(*b*) *It is superior to the Old Covenant* (ix. 1–x. 18).

(1) It is *heavenly*, *spiritual*, *eternal*, and has only *the shedding of blood* in common with the Old. It will *abide* while the Old passes away (ix.).

(2) It can *do more* for men, because it has a *perfect* and a *willing* Sacrifice, and therefore brings *complete forgiveness* (x. 1–18).

B.—Warnings and Exhortations

I.—*Three Warnings*, introduced as parentheses:

(*a*) If Jesus is greater than the old messengers, to hear His word brings *greater responsibility* (ii. 1–4).

(*b*) He is greater than *Moses* or *Joshua*. If we are unfaithful to Him, we shall lose a *better Canaan* than that lost by the Israelites who fell in the wilderness (iii. 1–iv. 13).

(*c*) If the writer is to speak of the greater privileges opened by them by Christ, they must be prepared to *exert* themselves *to go on to perfection* (v. 11–vi. 20).

II.—*Main Exhortation* (x. 19–xiii. 17).

(*a*) They must be *faithful* to the New Covenant, *using* its privileges, *dreading* unfaithfulness, and *repeating* their former endurance (x. 19–39).

(*b*) They have the examples of many *heroes and heroines of faith* and of *Jesus Himself* to encourage them (xi. 1–xii. 4).

(*c*) If they are true *sons* of God, they must expect *chastening* and must not forfeit their position (xii. 5–17).

(*d*) The glorious kingdom to which they now belong is *worth any sacrifice* (xii. 18–29).

(*e*) Their *daily life* must correspond to their great position (xiii. 1–17), even if it involves a painful *break with Judaism* (*vv.* 10–14).

CHAPTER XVII

The Epistle of James

This Epistle claims to be written by "James, a servant of God and of the Lord Jesus Christ." Two of the Twelve bore the name of James; but one was always called "James the brother of John," and was killed by Herod in A.D. 44 (Acts xii. 1, 2), and the other was always called "James the son of Alphæus," and was perhaps the same as "James the Less," which means either the little one or the younger (Mark xv. 40). If either of these was the writer, he would have described himself in full, and would probably have stated also that he was an Apostle. There was only one James in the Early Church, who was known as "James" simply, namely, *James the brother of Jesus*, often called "James of Jerusalem."

A.—THE LIFE OF JAMES, THE LORD'S BROTHER

It is a disputed question whether the "brethren" of Jesus were His *full brothers* as sons of Joseph and Mary, or His *stepbrothers* as sons of Joseph by a previous marriage, or merely His *cousins*. Except for sentiment there is no reason to deny that they were his full brothers, younger than Himself. Of the four, namely, James, Joseph,

Simon, and Judas, James is placed first (Matt. xiii. 55), and was presumably the eldest. They did not become disciples until after the Resurrection (John vii. 5); but they heard some of the teaching of Jesus (Matt. xii. 46), and were not hostile to Him. Jesus appeared to James after the Resurrection (1 Cor. xv. 7), and he and other members of the family joined the band of disciples in the upper room before Pentecost (Acts i. 14).

James very soon came to rank as at least the equal of the original Apostles: Paul calls him an Apostle (Gal. i. 19) and a "pillar" of the Church (Gal. ii. 9); he presided at the Council of Jerusalem (Acts xv. 13); his name carried weight in distant Churches, such as Antioch (Gal. ii. 12); and he was the leading authority in the Church of Jerusalem at the time of Paul's last visit (Acts xxi. 18). He is generally known as the first "Bishop" of Jerusalem.

There are many references in early Christian literature to his high character; and Josephus, the Jewish historian, makes it clear that even the unbelieving Jews held him in great reverence and called him "the Just." One tradition states that he was hurled from a pinnacle of the Temple by certain Jews whom he had angered by insisting that Jesus was the Christ. But Josephus states that Ananus, the high priest in A.D. 62, had him stoned quite illegally and in defiance of the protests of many of the citizens, and that he was deposed from the high-priesthood in consequence. Many of the Jews appear to have believed that the destruction of Jerusalem was the vengeance of Heaven for this crime.

B.—DID JAMES WRITE THE EPISTLE?

In many ways James was admirably suited to be the writer of this Epistle:

(*a*) His commanding position in Jerusalem would make it appropriate that he should send some message to the Churches generally.

(*b*) The Jewish tone of the Epistle is quite intelligible if he wrote it.

(*c*) As an independent hearer of Jesus he would be able to reproduce much of His teaching in rather different words from those of the Gospels.

(*d*) There is a close resemblance between the language of the Epistle and that of James's speech and the circular to the Gentile Churches in Acts xv. 13–29.

Those who date the Epistle late, of course, have to deny that James wrote it, though some think that it was compiled from his teaching somewhat after the style of a memorial volume. Apart from the matter of date, the only *objections* urged are that:

(*a*) He does not call himself the Lord's brother. But modesty would forbid this; and he would also remember that Jesus described as His brethren all those who do God's will (Matt. xii. 50).

(*b*) The Greek of the Epistle is good. But we have no right to assume that James's Greek would be bad, for Greek was freely spoken in the busier towns of Galilee, such as Capernaum.

C.—THE DATE OF THE EPISTLE

James may be dated either very early, say A.D. 50, or late, well after A.D. 70. Unfortunately the two main facts we have to guide us may be used as arguments for either date. The facts are these:

Circumcision Controversy.—There is no trace of the difference between Jewish and Gentile Christianity. This may mean that the Epistle was written before the question of circumcision arose, that is, before the Council of Jerusalem (A.D. 49 or 50), when James was in the thick of the controversy. Or it may mean that it was written when the dispute had died out, which was not until long after James's death, for his last interview with Paul, shortly before his death, had to do with this subject (Acts xxi. 17–25).

The earlier date is the more likely, for the Epistle is so Jewish that it suggests a time when the Church as a whole was still Jewish: it does not so much as hint that there was, or ever had been, any controversy concerning Gentile Christians.

New Testament parallels.—There are many parallels between James and Romans, Galatians, Hebrews and 1 *Peter, as well as with Matthew (or, perhaps, Luke).* If the writers of all these used James, it must have been written very early; but if the writer of James used them, it must be very late.

Once more the earlier date is the more likely. If James knew Matthew's or Luke's version of the Sermon on the Mount, we should expect him to reproduce not only many of the ideas, as he does, but much of the language, which he does not do. And if we compare James ii. 14–26 with Rom. iii. 21–iv. 3, James appears to give us a cruder, and therefore earlier, statement of the doctrine of Justification, which Paul seeks to improve upon.

Early date.—The *arguments in favour of an early date* are, therefore, as follows:

(1) To deny that it was written by James makes many serious difficulties. But if it was written by James, the latest possible date was A.D. 62, the year of his death.

(2) It appears to belong to a time before the Gentile question had arisen, i.e., before A.D. 50.

(3) It appears to have been used by several New Testament writers, and to be earlier than Galatians and Romans, which were written in A.D. 57 at the latest.

(4) There is no trace of any elaborate Church organization.

The only *objections* urged are that:

(1) The evils denounced point to great degeneration in the Church, and imply the lapse of many years. But the sin of Ananias and Sapphira occurred probably within less than a year of Pentecost, and the sins of the Corinthian Church developed within a very few years of its foundation.

(2) It was a long while before it was admitted to the Canon. But this was probably because it was addressed to no particular Church, so that no great Church would feel concerned to plead for it. Further, its Jewish tone and the meagreness of the distinctly Christian element would tend to create prejudice against it. Even Luther called it "an epistle of straw," and would not have regretted its absence from the New Testament.

The balance of argument is certainly in favour of the early date, and it was probably written in A.D. 49 or 50, the earliest of all the books of the New Testament.

It should be noted, however, that recent opinion, as represented by Burkitt and Kennedy, finds a considerable Hellenistic strain in the Epistle. Burkitt suggested that James may have written a tract for Jewish Christians in Aramaic, and that this, after being lost sight of for many years, was translated into Greek and brought up to date by Gentile Christians about A.D. 110.

D.—TO WHOM WAS THE EPISTLE WRITTEN?

Salutation.—The opening words read, "James . . . to the twelve tribes which are of the Dispersion." The "Dispersion" was a common description of the *Jews living outside Palestine.* This salutation has been interpreted in three ways:

(*a*) *Jews generally.*—The most obvious suggestion is that it refers to *Jews in general*, whether believing or unbelieving. The Jewish word "synagogue" is used for the assembly for worship (ii. 2), and the examples chosen are Jewish, e.g., the works of Abraham (ii. 21) and Rahab (ii. 25), the prayer of Elijah (v. 17), and the patience of Job (v. 11), instead of the sufferings of Christ.

This theory has taken two forms:

(1) It is said that it was *a purely Jewish tract*, written by a Jew and having no connexion with James, but that a few Christian touches were added to make it suitable for use in Christian worship, and that the name of James was then attached to it. But—(*a*) the Christian expressions are so firmly imbedded in the Epistle that they cannot have been inserted in this way: there are so many references to the teaching of Jesus that if they were removed

there would be nothing left. (*b*) If the writer had meant Jews alone to be his readers, he would have called them the twelve tribes *of Israel*.

(2) Dr. J. H. Moulton held that the Epistle was *by James*, but that it was meant for *unbelieving Jews*. Its first aim was not to make them Christians but to make them better Jews. Yet a great deal of the teaching of Jesus is introduced, and they would thus become familiar with it without knowing that it was His. This would prepare them to listen more sympathetically to Christian preaching afterwards. Such a theory would explain the scarcity of the distinctly Christian expressions. (Dr. Moulton supposed that in the original form of the Epistle even these were missing, and that what we have is a second edition prepared for Christian use.) It would also explain why the letter was so slowly recognized: it was too Jewish to be popular with Christians, and, on the other hand, Jews would cease to read it after James had been martyred as a Christian.

(*b*) *Jewish Christians.*—It is suggested that the writer had in mind *Jewish Christians outside Palestine*. James may well have wished to send some message to his believing countrymen in other parts. But in that case we should expect more references to their special needs and difficulties, for the sins condemned were not at all confined to Jewish Christians e.g., they all existed at Corinth, where the Church was almost entirely Gentile.

(*c*) *The new Israel.*—The salutation may refer to the *Christian Church*, *Jewish or Gentile*, *regarded as God's new Israel*, though at the time of writing it happened to consist almost entirely of those who had been Jews or proselytes. In favour of this we have the fact that Paul described the Christian Church in this way (Gal. vi. 16), and so did Peter (1 Peter i. 1). On this view the Jewish character of the Epistle and the Jewish examples of patience and faith are there, not because James thought that his only readers would be Jews, but because he himself was steeped in the Old Testament.

1. *Parallels with the Sermon on the Mount*

Almost the whole of the Sermon on the Mount is reproduced in James in somewhat different language. Note the following parallels with Matt. v.–vii. and the corresponding passages in Luke: James i. 2, 3, v. 10 = Matt. v. 10–12; Luke vi. 22, 23. James i. 5–8, 17, v. 16–18 = Matt. vii. 7–11, vi. 22; Luke xi. 9–13. James i. 9, ii. 5 = Matt. v. 3; Luke vi. 20. James i. 11 = Matt. vi. 30. James i. 13 = Matt. vi. 13. James i. 22–27, ii. 14–26 = Matt. vii. 22–27; Luke vi. 46–49. James ii. 8 = Matt. v. 43–48; Luke vi. 27–36. James ii. 13 = Matt. vi. 15; Luke vi. 37, 38. James iii. 8 = Matt. v. 9. James iii. 13 = Matt. v. 5. James iv. 4 = Matt. vi. 24; Lukc xvi. 13. James iv. 11, 12, v. 9 = Matt. v. 22, vii. 1–5; Luke vi. 37, 38. James iv. 14 = Matt. vi. 34. James v. 1–3 = Matt. vi. 19–21; Luke vi. 24, 25. James v. 12 = Matt. v. 34–37.

2. *Faith and Works*

A famous difficulty is raised by James ii. 14–26, for at first sight this passage seems directly to contradict Paul's teaching on the subject of Justification by Faith (Rom. iii. 21–iv. 3). But we shall feel little or no difficulty if we recognize that James and Paul attach very different meanings to the great words *faith*, *law*, and *works*.

(*a*) *Faith*. Paul means by this personal trust in Christ, and James recognizes that in this sense faith is the very essence of the Christian life (see James ii. 1). The faith which according to James cannot save us is a bare belief in the existence of God, such as even the devils have (ii. 19)—it is obvious that this does not necessarily make a man good.

(*b*) *Law*. When Paul says that "works of the law" are useless, he means the ceremonies of the Jewish Law. But when James urges obedience to the "law" he means the "law of liberty" (i. 25), that is, the law of Christian love and duty, which Paul also emphasizes in Gal. v. 13, 14, and in all his practical exhortations.

(*c*) *Works*. James means by "works" the acts of Christian conduct; Paul prefers to call these "the fruits of the Spirit" (Gal. v. 22), and retains the word "works" for Jewish ceremonies. Yet in 1 Thess. i. 3 even Paul speaks of the outcome of Christian faith as works, for "your work of faith" means the actions that spring from your faith.

Conclusion. Both Paul and James ask for an active, working faith, but their emphasis is a little different: Paul asks for a *faith* that works, and James asks for a faith that *works*.

OUTLINE OF JAMES

This Epistle touches upon so many different

topics that some suppose that James (or possibly some disciple of his) has given us brief summaries of a number of his sermons rather than an Epistle proper. It is difficult to outline satisfactorily, but the line of thought seems to be as follows:

Salutation (i. 1).

I.—*Consolation for the tempted and tried* (i. 2–18).
- (*a*) The *good results* which temptation and trial produce (i. 2–12).
- (*b*) The *origin* of temptation (i. 13–18).

II.—*A description of pure religion* (i. 19–iv. 12).
- (*a*) *It involves* doing as well as hearing (i. 19–27).
- (*b*) *It forbids:*
  - (1) Respect for wealth apart from character (ii. 1–13).
  - (2) A profession of faith without corresponding works (ii. 14–26).
  - (3) Rash or unbecoming speech (iii. 1–12).
- (*c*) *It produces:*
  - (1) Heavenly wisdom and gentleness (iii. 13–18).
  - (2) Spiritual desires and humility (iv. 1–10).
  - (3) Charity in our judgment of others (iv. 11, 12).

III.—*Warnings of death and judgment* (iv. 13–v. 11).
- (*a*) *Life is uncertain* (iv. 13–17).
- (*b*) *Judgment upon rich tyrants is sure* (v. 1–6).
- (*c*) *The End is near* (v. 7–11).

IV.—*Miscellaneous counsels* (v. 12–20).

CHAPTER XVIII

The First Epistle of Peter

A.—THE LIFE OF SIMON PETER

The Gospel story.—Simon was the brother of Andrew, and the son of a certain Jonas (Matt. xvi. 17), or John (John xxi. 15 R.V.). His original name was Simon, but Jesus added the name "Peter" (or in Aramaic "Cephas").

Both brothers were with John the Baptist at Jordan, and Peter was introduced to Jesus by Andrew (John i. 41). Jesus called them to definite discipleship some weeks, or even months, later, whilst they were at their work as fishermen near Capernaum (Matt. iv. 18–22). Peter was married and one of the early miracles of Jesus was to heal his wife's mother of a fever (Mark i. 30, 31). In after days his wife seems to have accompanied him on his preaching tours (1 Cor. ix. 5).

Peter, James, and John were present at the raising of the daughter of Jaïrus (Mark v. 37) and at the Transfiguration (Mark ix. 2), and they were also nearest to Jesus in Gethsemane (Mark xiv. 33).

Peter was of an impetuous disposition—eager to walk upon the sea (Matt. xiv. 28), the first to acknowledge Christ's full Divinity (Matt. xvi. 16), confident that he would not prove disloyal (Mark xiv. 29–31), ready with his sword in the Garden (John xviii. 10), running eagerly and entering boldly into the empty Sepulchre (John xx. 3–6), and swimming hastily to shore to see Jesus (John xxi. 7). But like many impulsive men, he lacked stability and real courage, hence his shameful denial of his Lord (Mark xiv, 66–72). The oaths and curses used on that occasion suggest that he had probably been given to coarse and foul speech in his earlier days.

After the Resurrection Jesus met him privately (1 Cor. xv. 5), and a little later at the lakeside Peter atoned, publicly for his threefold denial by a threefold assurance of his love for Jesus (John xxi. 15–17).

Christ's promise.—Special note must be made of Peter's great confession of faith in Christ at Cæsarea Philippi, and the striking promises made to him by Jesus (Matt. xvi. 15–19). It is on these words that the Roman Catholics base their assertion that the only true Church rests on Peter, and that the only valid Ministry is that which descends by direct succession from him. They also assert that Peter can admit to or exclude from Heaven. The real meaning of the promise seems to be as follows:

(1) Peter was the "rock" upon which Christ built his Church in the sense that the first believers on the Day of Pentecost based their faith on Peter's testimony concerning Him. But in view of 1 Cor. iii. 11, many suppose that the actual foundation was that faith in Christ's Divinity which Peter had just confessed, and that Peter as the earliest

to confess this faith was the first stone built on to the foundation.

(2) He had "the keys of the Kingdom of Heaven" in the sense that it was his privilege at Pentecost to declare the Kingdom open and invite men to enter it through faith in Christ. (Note that Christ did not promise him the keys of *Heaven*, but the keys of the *Kingdom* of Heaven—a very different matter.)

(3) The power to "loose" (or allow) and "bind" (or forbid) means that Jesus gave him a certain authority to decide doubtful points that might arise in connexion with belief or conduct. But Jesus gave precisely the same authority to the disciples generally (Matt. xviii. 18), and it amounts to no more than this—that when we are in doubt as to whether a certain doctrine is true, or perplexed as to whether it is right to do some particular thing, we can find no better guide than the judgment of a company of Christian people carefully and prayerfully given. Such a judgment is not by any means infallible, but it is as nearly correct as any decision can be, and God expects us to regard it as a kind of standard for practical purposes. Similarly, no Christian father is infallible, yet his will is the standard of right which God expects a child to accept (Eph. vi. 1), because his judgment is more likely to be correct than that of the child.

That Christ did not confer upon Peter the unique position claimed for him by the Romanists is clear from the following facts:

(1) Jesus denounced him as "Satan" almost immediately after uttering the great promise (Matt. xvi. 23).

(2) In 1 Peter ii. 4–6 Peter himself describes *Christ* as the great "Corner Stone," and *all* believers as "living stones."

(3) Neither Peter nor any one else in the early days seems to have imagined that he occupied any unique position in the Church, e.g., James soon became a greater authority at Jerusalem.

Acts and Epistles.—Continuing the story of Peter after the Ascension we find that he took the lead at Pentecost: he delivered the first sermon (Acts ii. 14), and worked the first miracle (iii. 6); he and John were brought before the Council (iv. 1–21); and he pronounced judgment on Ananias and Sapphira (v. 1–11). Paul met him on his first visit to Jerusalem after his conversion, and stayed with him fifteen days (Gal. i. 18). He visited the newly founded Churches of Samaria (Acts viii. 14), healed Æneas at Lydda, and restored Dorcas to life at Joppa (ix. 32–43). An event of very far-reaching importance was the vision at Joppa (x. 9–16), and the admission of Cornelius into the Church as the first *uncircumcised* Christian (x. 17–48). Peter was thus the earliest champion of Gentile Christianity (xi. 1–18).

He was condemned to death by Herod, but an angel opened the prison gates, and he escaped (xii. 3–17). He went to the house of Mary, the mother of Mark, a foreshadowing of the days when Mark would be his companion and put his Gospel into writing. Luke tells us that Peter then "went to another place" (*v.* 17). According to the Romanists it was at this time that he went to Rome and entered upon a twenty-five years' ministry there (see p. 154). It is most probable that he went to Antioch and other towns not very far from Jerusalem, for he was present at the Council of Jerusalem (Acts xv. 7), and the next we hear of him is that Paul rebuked him at Antioch for yielding to his old Jewish prejudices and refusing to eat with Gentiles (Gal. ii. 11).

The New Testament tells us nothing more of him except that he wrote this Epistle from "Babylon," i.e., Rome, almost certainly about the year A.D. 64. We gather from Papias that Mark was with him there about this time, and wrote the Gospel as a summary of Peter's teaching concerning Jesus (see pp. 21, 41). There is no doubt that both Peter and Paul were martyred there, but it is not certain which died first.

Dates.—Dr. Chase in Hastings's *Dictionary of the Bible* gives the following dates:

A.D. 29–35. Ministry in Jerusalem and Samaria.

A.D. 35–44. Missionary journeys, including somewhat lengthy stays at Lydda, Joppa, and Cæsarea, with several visits to Jerusalem.

A.D. 44–61. Work in Syria with Antioch as a centre; at least one visit to Jerusalem (Acts xv. 7).

A.D. 61–64. Work at Rome, with probably one visit to Jerusalem. Martyred shortly after the Fire at Rome in July, A.D. 64.

Traditions.—Early literature abounds in traditions concerning Peter, a few of them very beautiful, but many of them altogether fanciful and impossible. There is hardly any locality where

Christianity existed in the early centuries which does not claim to have been visited by Peter; and a whole series of apocryphal books was ascribed to him, the best known being the *Gospel of Peter*, the *Apocalypse of Peter*, and the *Preaching of Peter*. The collision with Paul at Antioch was so magnified by tradition that according to the critics of eighty or ninety years ago the history of the Early Church consisted almost entirely of a bitter rivalry between the two Apostles and the "parties" they established. This theory is quite fantastic. Both the Apostles were certainly in Rome about A.D. 64, and apparently on friendly terms; and Peter was so far from regarding Paul as his enemy and rival that he appears to have made use of Romans and Ephesians in writing this Epistle.

B. THE AUTHORSHIP OF I PETER

Peter.—The external evidence is very good, and it is so generally acknowledged that the Epistle was written by Peter that there is little need to discuss the question. This belief is confirmed by a number of references in the Epistle:

1. *The writer claims to have been an eye-witness of the Saviour's life and death:* e.g., in the words, "Whom having not seen *ye* love" (i. 8), he contrasts the readers' case with his own; and he calls himself "A witness of the sufferings of Christ" (v. 1).

2. *Several facts point directly to Peter:* e.g., (1) the figure of the Corner Stone and the "living stones" (ii. 4–6) would be suggested by Christ's great promise to him. (2) He describes Christ as

the "Shepherd" (ii. 25) and the "chief Shepherd" (v. 4), and bids the elders "Tend the flock of God" (v. 2), expressions which would be suggested to him by Christ's words, "Feed My sheep" and "Tend My sheep" (John xxi. 15–17).

Some *objections* have been raised:

1. Chapter iv. 12–19 seems to indicate *widespread persecution by the Roman Government*, and it is objected that this did not begin within Peter's lifetime. It is true that in Nero's time Christians were not supposed to be condemned merely because they were Christians, but only because they were accused of setting fire to Rome. But seeing that *every* Christian was included under this charge, the mere fact of being a Christian actually brought great peril in Rome, and there may have been similar persecutions in Asia Minor. The words "fiery trial" (iv. 12) seem particularly appropriate when we remember that in the year A.D. 64 Nero was using the Christians as "human torches" to illuminate his gardens. On the subject of this persecution see page 224.

2. *The Greek of the Epistle is better than we should expect from Peter*, especially as Papias tells us that Mark had to serve as his "interpreter." But Silvanus (i.e., Silas) acted as Peter's scribe in writing this Epistle (v. 12), and he was perfectly familiar with Greek.

3. *There are many parallels with Romans, Ephesians and James.* But if, as many believe, "Testimonies," or lists of proof-texts, etc., were widely used at a very early date (see p. 22), Peter might well quote many of the same Old Testament passages as Paul

and James, without drawing upon their Epistles. Yet there is no reason why Peter should not have known these Epistles and used them. Even those who date our "James" very late suppose that James himself wrote a Jewish-Christian tract which became the basis of that Epistle, and, if so, Peter would almost certainly know it well. Romans had also been written some seven or eight years; and further, the great doctrines of salvation were not a monopoly of Paul's, for he had talked them over with Peter and the other leaders many years before (Gal. ii. 2). As to Ephesians, that was written very shortly before the supposed date of this Epistle, and Peter and Paul were both in Rome at the time, so that it is not at all surprising that there should be some parallels, in fact they confirm the genuineness of both Epistles. (Compare especially the teaching of the two on the duties of servants, wives, and husbands.)

C.—THE READERS AND THEIR CIRCUMSTANCES

Gentiles.—The greeting reads, "To the elect who are sojourners of the Dispersion in Pontus, Galatia, Cappadocia, Asia, and Bithynia." As we saw in the case of James, the word "Dispersion" does not necessarily imply that they were Jews, but rather means that Peter thought of the Christian Church as God's *new Israel* at present scattered abroad. Hence he describes them as God's chosen people (ii. 9). Several passages which mention a very evil past imply that they were originally *heathen* (i. 14, i. 18, iv. 2–4).

Asia Minor.—All the provinces named belong

to *Asia Minor*. A number of evangelists had preached to them, but not Peter himself (i. 12). Yet seeing that the multitude at Pentecost included visitors from Cappadocia, Pontus, Asia, and Phrygia, Christianity in these parts owed its origin to him. Much of this area was also touched by Paul in his journeys, and the Gospel would naturally spread from the Churches he founded into more remote districts, such as Pontus and Bithynia. The provinces are named here in the order in which Silas would visit them if he travelled from Rome through the Black Sea to Pontus, and then worked back towards Rome.

Persecution.—There are many references to *suffering and persecution.* It may have been organized persecution of Christians as such (iv. 12–16), but it is not certain that the Government was responsible for it, since much of their suffering appears to have been caused simply by the malice of evil-minded neighbours.

Date.—The date was almost certainly A.D. 64. It can hardly have been earlier, because of the parallels with Ephesians; and it can hardly have been later, for Peter was probably martyred that year.

D.—WHERE WAS THE EPISTLE WRITTEN?

"*Babylon.*"—"She that is in Babylon, elect together with you, saluteth you; and so doth Mark my son" (v. 13). There is no evidence that any Christianity existed in Babylon at this time, or that Peter ever went there. On the other hand, "Babylon" was used as a symbolic name for Rome (see Rev. xviii. 10), and it stands for Rome here. "She" can hardly refer to Peter's wife: it means the Church at Rome. Mark was of course Peter's "son" only in the spiritual sense.

Silvanus.—The Silvanus, or Silas, who acted as Peter's scribe and carried the letter, was almost certainly the same Silas who was a companion of Paul on some of his journeys (Acts xv. 40, etc.).

E. THE MEANING OF I PETER III. 18–21

"*The spirits in prison.*"—The New Testament is almost completely silent concerning the interval that Christ spent in the tomb. Rom. x. 7 and xiv. 9, and Eph. iv. 9 perhaps refer to the "descent into Hell" (or rather "Hades," the world of the dead); but it is directly mentioned only in Peter's sermon at Pentecost (Acts ii. 27 and 31) and here.

The passage is exceedingly obscure. The chief question is, who were "the spirits in prison"?

(1) They may have been the wicked to whom Noah preached in vain. In that case the passage means that when Noah appealed to them it was really the pre-existent Christ who spoke through him.

(2) The curious phrase "spirits in prison" reminds us of the Book of Enoch, which has a good deal to say of those "sons of God," or angels, who formed unions with the daughters of men (Gen. vi. 1–8). The Jews regarded them as spirits hopelessly fallen. The Book of Enoch states that Enoch preached to them, and it is very probable that what Peter wrote in verse 19 was, "In which also *Enoch* went," etc. A very simple slip on the part of the scribe would change this into our present reading.

(3) The spirits in prison may be all the wicked who had passed away before Christ's coming, and Peter may mean that to meet their case Christ preached to them in this interval.

The theory of a future probation for the impenitent has been built up on this passage. But it is so obscure and so little supported by other Scripture that it does not provide a sufficient foundation for any theory of the future. Even if the third interpretation is correct, which is exceedingly doubtful, the most we can infer is that a further opportunity was given to those who had died in their sins *before* Christianity came into the world. It does not warrant us in supposing that there is a second probation for those who persist in sin in the full light of Christian knowledge.

OUTLINE OF I PETER

Greeting (i. 1, 2).

I.—*The privilege and responsibility of being Christians* (i. 3–ii. 10).

(*a*) They have hope and joy through Christ (i. 3–12).

(*b*) They have been redeemed at great cost that they may become holy (i. 12–25).

(*c*) They are God's new chosen people, or Israel (ii. 1–10).

II.—*They must show the Christian character by their conduct* (ii. 11–iii. 22).

(*a*) Pure in life (ii. 11, 12).

(*b*) Law-abiding as citizens (ii. 13–17).

(*c*) Faithful and submissive as servants (ii. 18–25).

(*d*) Chaste and simple as wives (iii. 1–6).
(*e*) Considerate as husbands (iii. 7).
(*f*) Patient under wrong (iii. 8–13).

III.—*They must be willing to suffer for righteousness' sake* (iii. 14–iv. 19).

(*a*) Christ suffered innocently, and now reigns in glory (iii. 14–22).
(*b*) God is to be their Judge, not their heathen neighbours (iv. 1–6).
(*c*) The End is near: they must make the most of the time that remains (iv. 7–11).
(*d*) The present persecution should not cause them dismay; it is an opportunity to glorify God (iv. 12–19).

IV.—*Miscellaneous counsels* (v. 1–11).

Conclusion (v. 12–14).

CHAPTER XIX

Second Peter and Jude

A.—THE CONNEXION BETWEEN 2 PETER AND JUDE

1. *The common section*

It is necessary to consider these two Epistles together, because of the extraordinary fact that almost the whole of Jude is found in 2 Peter ii. This section appears a little more fully in Jude, and consists of a fierce denunciation of certain heretical characters. They denied Christ (Jude 4); they were grossly immoral like the men of Sodom (Jude 7); they derided the Church authorities (Jude 8); and they were as covetous and mercenary as Balaam (Jude 11). In their immorality they were fore-runners of those monstrous *Antinomian* sects, which at a later date repudiated the moral law in the name of Christianity, and adandoned themselves to every vice on the plea that the Christian man is "free," In their theological speculations and their claim to be intellectually superior to orthodox Christians we have the beginnings of *Gnosticism*.

We have no clue to the locality to which either of the Epistles was addressed; but in view of the hold that the Colossian heresy obtained in A.D. 61 or 62, a double heresy of this crude kind might easily have existed in many parts of Asia Minor in A.D. 70–80.

2. *Which was original?*

It is quite clear from the very close agreement in this section that one Epistle has borrowed from the other, and there is little doubt that Jude was the original.

(1) If the author of Jude copied from 2 Peter, it is difficult to see why he should copy nothing from chapters i. and iii.

(2) If the author of 2 Peter copied from Jude, we can readily understand his omitting the references to Jewish legends and apocryphal books which might prejudice Christian readers. We can also understand his toning down some of Jude's stronger phrases, and his addition of more helpful teaching, so that the Epistle should not consist of mere invective and denunciation.

B.—THE SECOND EPISTLE OF PETER

1. *The authorship of 2 Peter*

The writer's claim.—This is the one book of the New Testament whose genuineness is a serious problem. In the cases of Matthew and Hebrews, though the *authorship* is uncertain, no question of *genuineness* arises, for Matthew does not claim to be by Matthew, nor does Hebrews claim to be by Paul. But 2 Peter does claim to be by the Apostle Peter (i. 1), and the writer also asserts that he had been a witness of the Transfiguration (i. 17, 18), and that he had written a previous Epistle (iii. 1).

Objections.—There is no denying that there is

practically no evidence in favour of this claim, and a great mass of evidence against it.

(*a*) *No definite mention of the Epistle is found before Origen* (A.D. 230). It is true, of course, that some Epistles which were written early, e.g., James, were slow in winning general recognition. It is also possible that some early writers used this Epistle without mentioning the writer. But there is the serious fact that the three most important references to it in the first four centuries (Origen, Eusebius, and Jerome) all state that it was *very doubtful* whether it was by Peter.

(*b*) As we have seen, 2 *Peter* ii. *seems to be copied from Jude*. If Peter knew the Epistle of Jude, he would probably not hesitate to use it, for some believe that he used Romans and Ephesians in writing 1 Peter (see p. 222). But there is this great difficulty—that Jude was probably not written until *long after Peter was dead*.

(*c*) *There is no resemblance between this Epistle and* 1 *Peter*. It is not merely that the language is different; the subjects and the general character of the message are different. In 1 Peter the danger is persecution, here it is heresy. The Greek of this Epistle is also very peculiar.

(*d*) *Some of the references point to a time later than Peter's death.*

(1) The Epistles of Paul (or some of them) had been collected and were regarded as "Scripture" in the same sense as the Old Testament (iii. 15, 16). This was certainly not the case when Peter died in A.D. 64.

(2) The first preachers of Christianity had been

so long dead that they were spoken of as "the fathers" (iii. 4).

(3) So long a time had passed without Christ's Second Coming that some had ceased to expect it (iii. 4).

(*e*) *A number of apocryphal books are known to have been ascribed to Peter* (see p. 221); it would not be very surprising if one of these was accepted by the Early Church in mistake.

Perhaps no one of these objections would be really fatal if it stood alone, but taken together they are very formidable. What is almost more serious is that there is nothing strongly in favour of Peter to be set against them. It would not even help very greatly if we supposed that Peter wrote chapters i. and iii., and that chapter ii. was inserted later, for serious difficulties would still remain.

The most that can be urged seems to be, as Pullan says, that the Early Church was probably in a better position to judge of the matter than we are, and it decided in favour of Peter's authorship. Yet that decision was given with extreme hesitation, for it was not till very late that it was admitted to the Canon, and then "only as a C3 recruit," so that even if we do not positively deny that the Epistle was by Peter, there is too little evidence for us to have the right to quote it as Peter's. For instance, it would not be fair in an argument to claim Peter's authority for any of its statements.

2. *The value of 2 Peter*

The conclusion is almost universal that the Epistle was not by Peter, and was not written until about A.D. 130. Even if we do not commit ourselves to this view, we have to ask, *What value can we attach to the Epistle seeing that the authorship is so doubtful?*

Is it a forgery?—At the worst it would not be a forgery in the modern sense of the word. The feeling in such matters at that time was hardly the same as our own. Where a modern writer acknowledges his debt to his teacher by a few words in the preface or by dedicating the book to him, a writer of that period would sometimes do it by effacing himself and sending forth his book in his master's name, as being the fruit of his teaching.

Historical value.—It throws light on the life and belief of the Church at the time at which it was written. For instance, the statements of this Epistle concerning the inspiration of the Old Testament (i. 16–21), and the end of the world (iii. 10–12), are of very great interest and value, even if we cannot claim for them the authority of Peter.

Spiritual worth.—It contains a number of *very beautiful and deeply impressive passages*, which are worthy to rank with any teaching of the New Testament. A surprising number of favourite texts and quotations come from this Epistle, for instance, i. 3, i. 4, i. 5–7, i. 10, 11, i. 16, iii. 13, iii. 18. In fact, in spite of the doubt about its authorship, it is of far greater spiritual value than Jude, about which there is much less question.

OUTLINE OF 2 PETER

Salutation (i. 1).

I.—*Prayer* (i. 2–4).

II.—*Exhortation to earnest moral effort* (i. 5–21).
(1) Spiritual progress requires effort (i. 5–11).
(2) It is the chief interest of his life to maintain their zeal (i. 12–15).
(3) They cannot doubt the truth of Christianity, for it is witnessed to by the Transfiguration and by the Old Testament prophets (i. 16–21).

III.—*Warning against false teaching* (ii.).
False teachers will arise as surely as in Old Testament times, and will lead men astray with the same disastrous results.

IV.—*Exhortations to watchfulness and diligence* (iii.).
(1) The promise of Christ's Coming still remains in spite of the delay (iii. 1–7).
(2) The End will come suddenly (iii. 8–13).
(3) The writings of Paul confirm this belief (iii. 14–18).

Doxology (iii. 18).

C.—THE EPISTLE OF JUDE

1. *Who was Jude?*

The writer calls himself, "Judas, a servant of Jesus Christ, and brother of James" (*v.* 1). In addition to Iscariot there was a second Judas among the Twelve, called "Judas of James" (Luke vi. 16), who was probably the same as Thaddæus (Matt. x. 3). He cannot have written this Epistle, for (1) the writer makes no claim to be an Apostle; (2) he distinguishes himself from the Apostles (*v.* 17); (3) the natural meaning of "Judas of James" is not *brother* of James, but *son* of James.

There was one man, however, in the Early

Church who would be recognized at once as "Judas the brother of James," namely the fourth of the brethren of our Lord (Matt. xiii. 55). We know little of him except that, like James, he was not a disciple until after the Resurrection. He was married (1 Cor. ix. 5) and died before the year A.D. 81, for in that year his grandsons, who were working men, were brought before the Emperor as some of the last surviving representatives of the line of David (see p. 56).

2. *Authorship and Date*

Date.—Some attempts have been made to show that the Epistle must be later than Jude's death. The writer uses some of Paul's Epistles, but he might very well do that in A.D. 70. He refers to two apocryphal books, but they were both in existence long before this date. Further, the heresy condemned was so crude that it might easily exist in A.D. 70. Hence there is nothing in the Epistle that might not have been written by Jude if he lived till, say, A.D. 70.

Author.—There is nothing in the Epistle to prevent us from believing that Jude wrote it; and we are left wondering how it ever came to be associated with him if he did not write it. Considering the shortness of the Epistle and the strangeness of its subject, the references in early writers are quite as numerous as we have any right to expect.

3. *References to Apocryphal Books*

This Epistle is remarkable for its references to certain Jewish myths (e.g., *v.* 9), and for its use of two Jewish apocryphal books, *The Assumption of Moses*, which appeared about A.D. 30, and the *Book of Enoch*, published some time in the century before the Birth of Christ. The latter professed to record prophecies delivered by Enoch!

OUTLINE OF JUDE

Salutation (*v.* 12).

I.—*A warning against the false teachers* (*vv.* 3–16).

(1) They are already at work (*vv.* 3, 4).

(2) History shows that apostasy brings a terrible penalty (*vv.* 5–11), e.g.: Unbelieving Israel (*v.* 5), the fallen angels (*v.* 6), Sodom and Gomorrah (*v.* 7), Cain, Balaam, Korah (*v.* 11).

(3) The false teachers are a plague to the Church, and a terrible destiny awaits them (*vv.* 12–16).

II.—*Exhortation to loyalty to the truth and purity* (*vv.* 17–23).

Doxology (*vv.* 24, 25).

CHAPTER XX

The Epistles of John

A.—THE FIRST EPISTLE OF JOHN

1. *Connexion with the Fourth Gospel*

Parallels.—This Epistle does not name its writer, but almost every verse reminds us of the Fourth Gospel. In both Jesus is the *Word* and the *only-begotten Son* of God; and if in the Gospel He is the *Lamb of God* that taketh away the sins of the world, in the Epistle He is the *propitiation* for the sins of the whole world. In both there is the same contrast between *God* and the *world*, and between *light* and *darkness*. In both the supreme revelation concerning God is His *love*, and the one duty of man is to fulfil the *new commandment* of *love*. In both the Christian experience is a *new birth* followed by *abiding in Christ*, and is the beginning of *eternal life*.

There are, of course, words and ideas in the Epistle which do not occur in the Gospel, but they are fully accounted for by the difference in aim of the two books.

Hence comparatively few doubt that both are by the same author; and if we are satisfied that the Gospel was by John the Apostle, we can have little hesitation in ascribing the Epistle to him also.

Order.—There is no certain clue as to which was

written first. As both were probably written in John's far old age, the interval must have been very short. It is perhaps more likely that the Gospel was written first, for the teaching of the Epistle seems to rest upon the Gospel, and it appears to be the practical exhortation to which the Gospel leads up, as if having set forth a particular view of the *life of Christ*, the writer wished now to describe the *life of the Christian* from the same standpoint.

2. *The authorship of* 1 *John*

Internal evidence.—The Epistle itself confirms the belief that it was written by John the Apostle:

(1) The parallels with the Gospel make it almost certain that both books were by the same author.

(2) The writer claims emphatically that he saw the earthly life of Christ (i. 1–3).

(3) He was so aged that he addresses all his readers as "Little children."

(4) John is believed to have spent his old age in Ephesus, the neighbourhood in which the heresy referred to first appeared.

External evidence.—The Epistle is consistently quoted as the work of John from very early days onwards. The Alogi, of course, rejected it, because like the Gospel, it teaches that Jesus was the Logos or Word of God; but apart from this the early belief was quite unanimous.

The title.—There is, however, one curious difficulty: Augustine several times calls it "The Epistle of John *to the Parthians*." But all the associations of the Epistle are with Ephesus and its neighbourhood: the heresy condemned belonged to that district, and the earliest traces of the use of the Epistle are found there. And except for the fact that visitors from Parthia were present at Pentecost, there is no evidence at all of the existence of Christianity so far east as Parthia at any early date. It is probable that Augustine misread some early description of the Epistle, e.g., he may have seen it called the Epistle to the *Patmians* or to the *Sardians*. Or, again, the Greek word for virgin (*parthenos*) is very similar to "Parthians." It so happens that, either because he was unmarried or because of his holy life, John was sometimes known as the "virgin." Augustine perhaps saw the Epistle described as the "Epistle of John *the Virgin*," or "the Epistle of John *to Virgins*" (which might possibly mean men and women of consecrated life). If so, a very slight error in reading would lead him to call it the Epistle to the Parthians.

Date.—All traditions refer both the Epistle and the Gospel to John's old age, and the references to the heresy make it impossible to date either of them earlier than A.D. 80–85. The general opinion inclines to A.D. 90–95, the Epistle being probably a little the later.

3. *The heresy condemned*

There is no purely doctrinal section and little theological argument in this Epistle. References to doctrine are indirect, and John seeks to guard his readers from error by emphasizing the truth rather than by discussing the heresy. Yet it is clear that he regarded very seriously the tendency *to deny the real Humanity of Jesus*. To-day many are so sure of the Humanity of Jesus that they can hardly believe in His Divinity, but at that time some were so sure of His Divinity that they could hardly believe in His real Humanity. In the second century many held that the body of Jesus was a mere *appearance* or *phantom*. This heresy was known as *Docetism*, from the Greek word meaning to seem or to appear.

This dangerous error is hinted at in the Gospel, for whilst that book lays the emphasis on Christ's Divinity, there are some very striking statements concerning His Humanity (see pp. 72, 73). In this Epistle the statements are even more emphatic. Note the following:

i. 1: That which we have *heard*, that which we have *seen* with our *eyes*, that which we *beheld*, and our hands *handled* concerning the Word of life.

iv. 2: Every spirit which confesseth that Jesus Christ is come in the *flesh* is of God.

v. 6: This is He that came by *water* and *blood*, even Jesus Christ; not with the *water* only, but with the *water* and with the *blood*.

As far as doctrine is concerned, the chief aim of the Gospel was to show that *Jesus was the Christ*; in the Epistle the aim was rather too show that *the Christ was Jesus*, a real Man.

4. *The spiritual teaching of* 1 *John*

The main purpose of the Epistle is not doctrinal, but practical; it is chiefly concerned with *the inner life of the Christian*, just as the Gospel was concerned with *the inner life of Jesus*. It describes what Paul calls the "life hid with Christ in God," and its main subject is the Christian's union with God through Christ, or fellowship in the Life Eternal. It is thus intensely *spiritual* and *mystical*. At the same time it is intensely *practical*, for the writer insists continually that love for God and union with God must manifest themselves in active deeds of love for men.

OUTLINE OF I JOHN

Subject: Fellowship in the Life Eternal.

I.—*Fellowship with God who is Light.*

(*a*) The writer's experience shows that it is possible (i. 1–4).

(*b*) It depends on walking in the light (i. 5–7).

(*c*) It must be gained through confession of sin, forgiveness, and obedience (i. 8–ii. 6).

(*d*) It requires a loving heart (ii. 7–11).

Warnings against—

1. Love of the world (ii. 12–17).
2. Antichrist and false doctrine (ii. 18–29).

II.—*Fellowship with God who is Righteous* involves:

(*a*) Purity of heart and active goodness (iii. 1–10).

(*b*) A loving heart and practical charity (iii. 11–24).

Warning against "false spirits," whose characteristic is worldliness (iv. 1–6).

III.—*Fellowship with God who is Love* involves:

(*a*) A deep sense of God's love (iv. 7–10).

(*b*) Love to God and to one another (iv. 11–21).

IV.—*Fellowship with God is union with God.*

(*a*) It produces:

(1) Love of the brethren (v. 1, 2).

(2) Victory over the world (v. 3–6).

(*b*) *It is assured to us* by the witness of the Spirit (v. 7–12).

(*c*) *It promises us:*

(1) Eternal life (v. 13).

(2) Limitless resources through prayer (v. 14–16).

(3) Deliverance from sin (v. 18-21).

B.—THE SECOND EPISTLE OF JOHN

1. *The author of 2 John*

"*The Elder.*"—The author calls himself simply "the Elder." Hence it is a fairly common belief that he was John the Presbyter. Yet it does not necessarily follow, for it is not quite certain that there was any such person, and John the Apostle had as much right to call himself an elder as the Archbishop of Canterbury has to call himself a clergyman. The Epistle was commonly accepted in the Early Church as the work of the Apostle.

Parallels with 1 John.—In favour of this view we find a surprising number of parallels with 1 John, for many of the most characteristic ideas and phrases of the first Epistle occur here, e.g., the truth abiding in us (*v.* 2), "Jesus Christ, the Son of the Father" (*v.* 3), walking in truth (*v.* 4), the new commandment of love (*vv.* 5, 6), deceivers and Antichrist (*v.* 7).

The Epistle is so brief and unimportant that its authorship is not a matter of great moment, but in view of the evidence we are fully justified in ascribing it to the Apostle.

2. *To whom was 2 John addressed?*

"*The elect lady.*"—The opening words read, "The elder unto the elect lady and her children." There are two possible interpretations:

(*a*) It may be written to *some Christian lady and her family*. In this case we should expect the writer to name her and to name the members of her family whom he had met in other parts (*v.* 4). and also the sister (*v.* 13). If the reference is to a particular lady, the address seems somewhat stilted, especially as in 3 John the writer, who was presumably the same, mentions several individuals by name.

(*b*) It may be written to *a Church and its members*. The "children" of verse 4 would then be members of this Church whom the writer had met elsewhere, and the "elect sister" of verse 13 would be the Church in his own locality.

OUTLINE OF 2 JOHN

Salutation (*vv.* 1–3).
- (*a*) *The writer's satisfaction* with the "children" he had met (*v.* 4).
- (*b*) *Exhortation* to faithfulness to the Christian ideal (*vv.* 5, 6).
- (c) *Warning* to beware of false teachers and to refuse to receive them (*vv.* 7–11).

Conclusion (*vv.* 12, 13).

C.—THE THIRD EPISTLE OF JOHN

1. *The author of 3 John*

There are so many links with 2 John that it is impossible to doubt that the two Epistles are by the same writer. He calls himself "the elder," verse 4 is very similar to 2 John 4, and the conclusion is almost word for word the same as that of the second Epistle. The chief message (*vv.* 5–8) also corresponds closely to that of 2 John, for if there we have a warning against entertaining false teachers, we have here an encouragement to show hospitality to true teachers.

As it seems most probable that the second Epistle was written by the Apostle, it is natural to ascribe this to him also.

2. *The persons named*

Gaius,—Gaius, to whom the letter is addressed, was evidently a man of some position, presumably in one of the smaller Churches of Asia Minor. He seems to have entertained the preachers and other Christians who visited the place from time to time. The New Testament mentions a Gaius of Macedonia (Acts xix. 29), a Gaius of Derbe (Acts xx. 4), and a Gaius of Corinth (1 Cor. i. 14; Rom. xvi. 23). But the name "Gaius" was so common that we should not be justified in identifying any of these three with the Gaius of this Epistle, especially if it was written late in the century.

Diotrephes.—Diotrephes was apparently an awkward and contentious member of the Church to which Gaius belonged. The writer had already addressed a letter to the Church concerning him (*v.* 9), but he evidently occupied too strong a position for the local members to control him, and the writer recognizes that he will have to come and deal with him personally (*v.* 10).

Demetrius.—Demetrius was a disciple of good report, perhaps the minister of the local Church, and it appears that Diotrephes had attacked him. The writer adds his testimony to his character. As the Church was probably somewhere in the neighbourhood of Ephesus, it has been suggested that "Demetrius the silversmith," who led the riot against Paul (Acts xix. 24–40), was now the Christian whom the writer so earnestly commends. But the name was very common, and so many years had elapsed that it is hardly likely that that Demetrius would still be living.

OUTLINE OF 3 JOHN

Salutation to Gaius (*v.* 1).

(*a*) *Personal matters* (*vv.* 2–8).

(1) The writer's good wishes (*v.* 2).

(2) His gratification at what he hears of Gaius (*vv.* 3, 4).

(3) Commendation of his hospitality (*vv.* 5–8).

(*b*) *Church matters* (*vv.* 9–12).

A condemnation of *Diotrephes*, urging Gaius to stand by *Demetrius*.

Conclusion (*vv.* 13, 14).

CHAPTER XXI

The Revelation or Apocalypse

A.—PROBLEMS OF THE REVELATION

The Revelation is the most perplexing book in the Bible. All that can be done in such a chapter as this is to state a few of the problems it suggests and refer briefly to some of the solutions that have been offered, for probably no one view of its origin and meaning will ever be accepted universally.

In every age a few have been fascinated by the very mystery of the book, especially by what they take to be its teaching on the subject of the Millennium, and for them it is almost the most precious part of the Bible. Others, from quite early days onwards, have been repelled by its obscurity and involved symbolism, and have virtually ignored the book. It is worthy of note that this was the attitude of the great Reformers: Luther declared at one time that it was neither apostolic nor prophetic, though he came to value it more highly afterwards; Zwingli asserted roundly that it was "not a Biblical book"; and Calvin deliberately omitted it from his commentary, as he also did 2 and 3 John. Even to-day the great majority of readers value it almost entirely for the sake of the letters to the Seven Churches and for some exquisitely beautiful passages on the subject of Heaven and the future life.

B.—APOCALYPTIC LITERATURE

Apocalypses.—The title is the *Apocalypse*, a word which means unveiling or revelation. Our Bibles call it "The Revelation of St. John the Divine," but the opening verse states that it is "the revelation of Jesus Christ, which God gave Him," i.e., it claims to be an unveiling of God and the things of God coming through Jesus Christ to John, and so to the world.

The name *Apocalypses* was given to a whole class of writings. In the Old Testament we have parts of Isaiah, Ezekiel, Daniel, and Zechariah. Others were *Fourth Esdras*, the *Book of Enoch*, the *Apocalypse of Baruch*, and, rather later, the *Apocalypse of Peter*.

Characteristics.—The *leading characteristics* of such books are that:

(1) They are not prophecy in the ordinary sense, for they refer more often to the solemn events of the End of the World than to forthcoming events in human history.

(2) Men and nations are not named directly, but are disguised under strange symbols, such as "beasts," "horns," etc.

(3) The mood of the writer is ecstatic; he claims to be describing visions, and the language is almost entirely figurative and poetic.

(4) The writer often assumes a fictitious name, e.g., the author of the Book of Enoch wrote as if he were the Enoch mentioned in Genesis, though

his book did not appear much before the birth of Christ.

This kind of literature makes little appeal to us to-day. But God appears to have used every form of expression to set forth His revelation of Himself; and as there are apocalypses in the Old Testament, it is hardly surprising that there should be one in the New.

C.—MATERIALS USED BY THE WRITER

Unity.—The book has a *very marked unity*: the theology and style are the same throughout, and no book in the New Testament is more carefully and methodically planned; so that whatever materials the writer may have used, he must have made them very completely his own before incorporating them.

Compilation. It would be as natural for the author to avail himself of existing apocalypses as it was for the writers of Kings and Chronicles to employ the different sources of information which they mention. There are two facts which are most easily accounted for by supposing that *some use was made of other books*:

(*a*) *Some parts seem to be Jewish in origin.* In chapter xi. 1, 2 it is implied that the Temple will remain when Jerusalem is destroyed. A Christian who had heard Jesus declare that not one stone should be left standing upon another could hardly be the original writer of this passage. Yet, if he found it in some existing Jewish apocalypse, he might take it over and use it as part of his symbolism.

(*b*) *The historical references perhaps cover a period of twenty-five years.* Some parts refer to Nero, who died in A.D. 68, and chapter xi. 1, 2 implies that Jerusalem was still standing. Other passages are taken by many to refer to the end of the reign of Domitian (A.D. 81–96).

Sources.—We can gather a little as to the *sources used*:

(*a*) Copious use is made of the symbolic portions of Ezekiel and Daniel.

(*b*) When the writer says that he "ate" the "little book" (x. 2, 8–10), he presumably means us to understand that he embodied it in his own book.

(*c*) He refers to another book with some such title as *The Apocalypse of the Seven Thunders*, which the angel apparently forbade him to use (x. 4).

It should be added, however, that those who are most confident that there has been compilation are quite unable to agree in their attempts to separate the different parts.

D.—DATE OF THE APOCALYPSE

The dates assigned to the book range from A.D. 70 to 96, whilst some suppose that parts of it were written even earlier than A.D. 70.

In support of the late date it is argued that:

(*a*) Some passages refer to the end of the reign of Domitian, A.D. 96.

(*b*) The worship of the Emperor is fully developed and persecution by the Government is almost universal, so that the Empire is described as the Great Harlot drunk with the blood of the martyred saints (xvii. 6). This is a great change from the time when Paul regarded the Empire as God's check upon sin (2 Thess. ii. 7, Rom. xiii. 1–7), and Peter enjoined obedience to its laws (1 Pet. ii. 13, 14, 17).

(*c*) The phrase "the Lord's day" (i. 10) has taken the place of the earlier phrase "the first day of the week" (1 Cor. xvi. 2).

(*d*) The terrible description of the hostile Jews as "the synagogue of Satan" (iii. 9) would hardly be possible at any early date.

In support of the earlier date it is argued that:

(*a*) The references are not necessarily to the reign of Domitian. English scholars, such as Hort and Lightfoot, as well as some even of the advanced continental critics, have found it possible to interpret all the historical references as applying to the earlier period.

(*b*) The terrible persecution under Nero, in which Peter and Paul both perished, would suffice to account for the change of feeling towards the Empire.

(*c*) It is quite likely that even if the book was published late it was written early and finished gradually.

The question of date is important, not only because it affects the meaning we attach to the historical references, but also because the style is so different from that of the Fourth Gospel that it is almost impossible to believe that both books were written by the same author *at the same period of his life*. Hence those who maintain that John the Apostle wrote both, and wrote the Gospel late, argue that the Apocalypse must have been written comparatively early, even if it was published later.

E.—THE AUTHORSHIP OF THE REVELATION

1. *The Alternatives*

Apostle or Elder?—There is great division of opinion concerning the Authorship, many ascribing it to *John the Presbyter or Elder*. Such a conclusion would certainly simplify a number of difficulties, but before accepting it we should remember that:

(*a*) *It is not certain that any such person ever existed.* Papias speaks of Aristion and the Elder John as early disciples of Jesus, and apparently means to distinguish this John from the Apostle. But he does not say that he lived at Ephesus. Dionysius (A.D. 255) states he had *heard* that there were two monuments at Ephesus to different Johns. Yet if he was so widely known that all the Churches of Asia recognized him by the name of "John" without further description, and if it was possible for him to assume the tone of authority found in this book, it is very surprising that we find no other traces of his existence.

(*b*) *There is absolutely no primitive testimony that he was the writer.* Dionysius (A.D. 255) argued that he was the author, but he did not bring forward a single earlier witness, and could only argue from the contents and style. His reasoning seems to have been this—the style makes it difficult to suppose that it was written by the author of the Gospel; there *appears* to have been another John; may not he have been the writer?

(*c*) Those who are most confident that there was a Presbyter John are more and more inclined to *deny that the Apostle was ever at Ephesus*, and to connect all the traditions with the Presbyter. If we had to admit this, very serious consequences would follow as regards the Gospel and Epistles.

If it proves really impossible to believe that the Apostle was the writer, the Elder will serve as a possible alternative. But we know nothing about him with any certainty, and the suggestion is a mere guess, with this advantage, however, over some others, that his name was John, and he was supposed to have been a disciple of Jesus.

2. *The Author's Statements concerning Himself*

The facts.—The writer tells us that his name was "John" (i. 1), and that he was a "servant" of God (i. 1), and a "brother" of his readers and a sharer in their persecutions (i. 9). He claims to have seen some, if not all, the visions as an exile or convict in Patmos, an island in the Ægean Sea (i. 9).

Estimate.—The Apostle alone would be likely to be known as "John" simply, and there is a tradition that he was banished to Patmos, though the traditions vary as to the date of this banishment.

Two facts are urged *against the Apostle*:

(*a*) The writer makes no claim to be an Apostle, and by the way in which he refers to the Twelve and their place in the future Kingdom (xxi. 14), he rather implies that he was not one of them. *But*—one who had asked for a place next to the throne of Jesus (Matt. xx. 21) would scarcely hesitate to picture the names of the Twelve, including his own, as graven on the foundations of the New Jerusalem.

(*b*) In the Gospel and Epistles the Apostle does

not name himself, yet the author of the Revelation mentions his own name several times. *But* —none of the Evangelists names himself as the author of his Gospel; and, on the other hand, it was imperative that any one who asked the Church to accept these amazing visions should name himself as the seer of them.

3. *The Testimony of Early Writers*

The facts. The Revelation was fairly widely quoted at an early date, and is frequently described as the work of "John" or "John the disciple." On the other hand, the first perfectly definite statement that it was by John the Apostle is not found until we reach Justin Martyr (A.D. 150), and in A.D. 255 Dionysius worked out in some detail the theory that it was by the Elder.

Estimate.—On the whole these facts favour the Apostle, for:

(*a*) A considerable section admitted it to their Canon quite early, i.e., they regarded it as apostolic

(*b*) If early writers did not think it necessary to specify which John they meant, it must have been because they referred to the best known of all the Johns, the Apostle.

(*c*) Dionysius was quite unable to bring forward any earlier witness in favour of the Elder, but could only argue from the style.

(*d*) The Alogi, who rejected it, evidently classed it with the Gospel and 1 John.

4. *Comparison with the Gospel and* 1 *John*

Parallels.—There are some very striking parallels with the Gospel and 1 John: (1) Christ is called "the Word" and "the Lamb," though the word for "Lamb" is not the same as that used in the Gospel. (2) There is the same attitude as in the Gospel towards the Jewish opponents of Christ-tianity, e.g., they are called "the synagogue of Satan" (iii. 9). (3) "The hidden manna" (ii. 17), reminds us of "the bread out of heaven" (John vi. 32), and the reference to "the water of life" (xxii. 17) is similar to John iv. 13, 14, vii. 37. (4) A number of other words characteristic of John are also used, e.g., "he that overcometh," "true," "truth," "keep," "witness," "testimony."

Estimate.—In favour of the Apostle it should be noted that these parallels include the great symbol "the Word," which is so absolutely peculiar to John that some think that it is almost sufficient by itself to connect this book with him.

Against the Apostle it may be said that: (1) There are fairly numerous parallels with the language of Paul. (2) There is little trace of some of John's favourite ideas concerning the Christian life, e.g., "light," "life," "love," and "abiding in Christ."

5. *The Style and Grammar*

Style.—By far the most perplexing feature of the problem is the *style*. (1) There are some very extraordinary and quite ungrammatical Greek expressions. (2) Even in the calmer and smoother passages there is little to remind us of John.

Dr. Selwyn in *The Christian Prophets* has attempted to represent in English some of the grammatical peculiarities of the Revelation, e.g.:

i. 4. From He that is, and He was, and He that cometh.

iii. 2. Stablish the last things which was about to die.

xiv. 14. And upon the cloud sitting one likened a Son of Man.

xvi. 14. For they is spirits of devils doing signs.

It is this matter of style which leads so many to assign the book to another author. Two explanations of the difference have been suggested:

(1) *The extraordinary character of the book called for extraordinary forms of expression.* Some suggest that they were introduced of set purpose, and that their very uncouthness makes them impressive, just as massive chords which violate the strict rules of music, and are really discords, may occasionally be used with great effect. It seems, however, that somewhat similar instances of faulty grammar occur in some of the documents unearthed in the Nile Valley. Further, it is not as if only a few special phrases were irregular; the grammar throughout is weaker than that of the Gospel.

(2) *There may have been a considerable interval between the two books.* An interval often produces a marked change of style and phrasing, e.g., in English literature we have the difference between the earlier and the later works of Ruskin.

It should be noted, however, that opinion moves more and more strongly to the later period, that of Domitian, as the setting for the Revelation. In this case the supposed interval in date between the two books almost vanishes, and the difficulty of believing that the Apostle could be the author of both becomes correspondingly greater.

At the same time, that difference of style does not necessarily prove difference of authorship is clear from the fact that so keen a critic as Harnack assigned all five books, the Gospel, the three Epistles, and the Revelation, to *one* writer, though he supposed him to have been the Elder. Hence the difference of style need not prevent those who believe that the Apostle wrote the Gospel from believing that he also wrote the Revelation.

Conclusion.—It is not quite impossible to accept the Revelation as the work of the Apostle, but the difficulties are so serious that we cannot feel certain on the matter. If we could be sure that there was a John the Presbyter, an original disciple of Jesus, living at Ephesus at the close of the century, and exercising a wide influence in the Churches of that district, it would remove many difficulties to suppose that he, and not the Apostle, was the author. Such a conclusion would not contradict any statement which the book makes concerning its author, and would not lessen its value.

F.—THE PURPOSE OF THE REVELATION

Purpose.—The *purpose* of the Revelation is clearly to comfort Christians under great persecution. This is done by the prophecy of the doom of the persecuting Empire, and by majestic descriptions of the final triumph of Christ and exquisite pictures of the happy destiny of the faithful.

"*The Seven Churches.*"—The address is to *the seven Churches of Asia* (i. 11). Seven Churches within the Roman province of Asia are named—Ephesus, Smyrna, Pergamum, Thyatira, Sardis, Philadelphia, and Laodicea—but the message is obviously through them to the whole Church. Other Churches existed in Asia, e.g., Colossæ, but seven were selected because seven was the Jewish "perfect number." In the same way we find seven revelations, seven choruses, seven seals, seven trumpets and seven bowls.

666.—The real meaning of the strange number 666 (xiii. 18) is almost certainly that 6 is less than 7, and therefore imperfect, so that 666 means trebly imperfect. To whom does it refer? Both in Greek and in Hebrew numbers were represented not by figures, but by letters. It was noticed at an early date that, by a curious coincidence, the figure-value of the Greek word for *Jesus* is 888, the superlatively perfect. The 666 may refer to Nero, for if *Nero-Cæsar* is written in Hebrew letters, the total comes to 666. It should be noted that Professor Charles, the foremost authority on apocalyptic literature. contends that the writer would expect his readers to think of the *Hebrew* letters. This interpretation would also account for the puzzling variant reading 616, which is found in some MSS. Nero's name was pronounced Nero (616) by those who spoke Latin, but Nero*n* (666) by those who spoke Greek. In stressing the 666 it is quite possible that the writer meant to emphasize the immeasurable contrast between the worship of the Emperor, 666, and the service of Jesus, 888.

The Mark of the Beast.—As to the "*mark* of the beast," Deissmann takes it to correspond to the "marks " or "seals" found on many of the *papyri.* They bore the date, and often the likeness of the Emperor, and were necessary on business documents. He suggests that during the persecution the seal was given a design or wording that amounted to Emperor-worship, and that Christians had to choose between giving up business and this kind of idolatry. Those who succumbed are pictured by the author of the Revelation not merely as using "the mark of the beast" on their bills, but as branded with it on their foreheads.

G.—LEADING IDEAS OF THE REVELATION

In spite of the general obscurity, five main prophecies stand out distinctly. But seeing that they are stated in the most highly symbolic and figurative language, we have no right to interpret them literally or to expect any exact fulfilment.

The fall of Rome is the subject in chapters xvi.–xviii. The first five bowls bring pestilence, the pollution of the sea, the pollution of the rivers, scorching heat, and then the darkening of the sun. As the writer speaks of Rome under the symbolic name of "Babylon," he naturally continues the figure and speaks of the River Euphrates. With the sixth bowl the Euphrates, which had prevented the approach of Babylon's enemies, is dried up, that is, the nations are allowed to gather for the great world battle at Har-Magedon (xvi. 16). The seventh bowl brings an earthquake, by which Babylon is divided into three parts (xvi. 17–19). Even then the city is still defiant, but its doom is certain (xvii. and xviii.)

There was, of course, no direct or literal fulfilment of this prophecy. Rome was sacked in A.D. 410 by the barbarian Goths, but before that date the Empire had become nominally Christian under Constantine, and official persecution had long ceased. The real fulfilment consisted in the breaking up of the opposition to Christianity.

The fall of Satan (xii.–xx.) carries us into the spirit-world. The writer pictures certain "beasts" or evil spirits which own allegiance to Satan, and which are the counterparts in the spirit-world of the Roman Empire and the system of Emperor-worship. Hence the ruin of the Empire is described as the fall of Satan, who was its real master (xx. 1–3). That is, the binding of Satan means the cessation of persecution.

The subject of the *Thousand years' reign of the Saints* or *Millennium* (xx. 1–6) has exercised an extraordinary fascination over many minds. Those who are known as *Millenarians*, or sometimes *Pre-millenarians*, look for a visible return of Christ resulting in the imprisonment of Satan and the reign of the saints *on earth* for a thousand years. After this they expect the release of Satan and the last great conflict between good and evil, leading up to *another* Return of Jesus, the resurrection of all the dead and the Judgment.

Only a crudely literal interpretation of an entirely symbolic and figurative book could warrant any such expectation, and it is not confirmed elsewhere in Scripture. The natural meaning is that with the downfall of Rome there would come a cessation of persecution, that is, a curbing of Satan's power, so that Christianity would be allowed to do its work freely. On this view the Millennium merely stands for the Church's freedom, since the worst forms of persecution ceased, and the "thousand years" merely indicates that it will be allowed this freedom for a long period. In other words, the Millennium is *now*, and in comparison with the conditions of that time our age *is* a golden Millennium.

The release of Satan (xx. 7–10). The period of the Millennium is a long one, yet it is not unlimited, and apparently we must not expect that the favourable conditions and the progress of Christianity will continue indefinitely. We cannot tell what form events will actually take, but Scripture leads us to suppose that before the End there will be something corresponding to what Paul calls the Great Apostasy and the Revelation of the Man of Sin (2 Thess. ii. 1–12), and what this book calls the release of Satan and the great final conflict.

A number of passages, some of them very beautiful, refer to the *Salvation of the Faithful*. Some of these have a Jewish cast, and might suggest that the writer expected a new Jerusalem to be established upon earth (xxi. 2). But others, e.g., chapter vii. 9–17, can only refer to the future life, so that the references to the "New Jerusalem" must be taken symbolically and spiritually.

OUTLINE OF THE REVELATION

The following outline is based upon that given in Pullan's *Books of the New Testament*, pp. 280–3. According to this the prophetical portion of the book includes seven revelations and seven choruses.

Introduction (i.–iii.).

1. Title and description (i. 1–3).
2. Vision of the Son of Man (i. 4–20).
3. Letters to the Seven Churches (ii., iii.).

First Revelation: The Lamb and the Book of Destiny (iv., v.).

1. Vision of the throne of God. *Chorus of creation* (iv.).
2. The sealed book. *Chorus of redemption* (v.).

Second Revelation: The Seven Seals, or Judgment threatened (vi. 1–viii. 1).

1. Six seals represent punishments held in check (vi.).
2. Sealing of the 144,000 and others. *Chorus of salvation* (vii.).
3. Seventh seal prepares for the next Revelation (viii. 1).

Third Revelation: The Seven Trumpets, or Judgment on Jerusalem (viii. 2–xi. 18).

1. Six trumpets introducing various chastisements (viii., ix.).
2. Relation of this to prophecy (x.).
3. Seventh trumpet announces the next Revelation. *Chorus of God reigning* (xi. 1–18).

Fourth Revelation: The Lamb's Redemption (xi. 19–xv. 4).

1. Christ's conflicts with the dragon, i.e., evil (xii.).
2. His conflict with the dragon's allies, i.e., Rome, etc. (xiii.).
3. The Lamb and His redeemed. The *incommunicable chorus*. Harvest of the world (xiv.).
4. *Chorus of Moses and the Lamb* (xv. 1–4).

Fifth Revelation: The Seven Bowls, or the Judgment of Rome (xv. 5–xix. 10).

1. Five different punishments on Babylon, i.e., Rome (xv. 5–xvi. 11).
2. Sixth bowl, leading to battle of all nations at Har-Magedon (xvi. 12–16).
3. Seventh bowl, partial destruction of Babylon (xvi. 17–21).
4. Further doom of Babylon and dirge over the city (xvii., xviii.).
5. *Triumphant chorus* (xix. 1–10).

Sixth Revelation: The Word of God and Universal Judgment (xix. 11–xx. 15).

1. Complete overthrow of Christ's enemies, the dragon, etc. (xix. 11–21).
2. Binding of Satan and the Millennium (xx. 1–6).
3. Release of Satan and his final defeat (xx. 7–10).
4. The Last Judgment (xx. 11–15).

Seventh Revelation: The New Jerusalem (xxi. 1–xxii. 5).

The City, the River of Life, the Tree of Life.

Conclusion (xxii. 6–21).

Solemn assertion of the truth of this Revelation.

It should be noted that the seven revelations are arranged with remarkable symmetry, for the fourth is the central message and the others are balanced one against the other in pairs on either side of it, thus:

I. II. III. IV. V. VI. VII.

The following table will perhaps make this clear:

I. The Lamb and the Book of Life.	. . . .	VII. The Lamb's Bride, New Jerusalem.
II. Judgment deferred.	. . . .	VI. Universal Judgment.
III. Judgment upon Jerusalem.	. . . .	V. Judgment upon Rome.
	IV. Redemption by the Lamb.	

Reading round in the order of the numbers, we get the sequence found in the book; reading across, each vision corresponds to its opposite.

Dr. James Moulton once remarked that the diagram at the foot of the previous page needs only a vertical line in the centre to form the Seven-Branched Candlestick, and that quite conceivably the author arranged his book with that in mind.

INDEX

BIBLICAL PASSAGES DISCUSSED

NOTES

NOTES

NOTES

NOTES

NOTES

NOTES

NOTES

NOTES

NOTES